There Came One Running

*The Hidden Story of
the Rich Young Ruler*

There Came One Running

The Hidden Story of the Rich Young Ruler

> And when he was gone forth into the way, there came one running, and kneeled to him, and asked him, "Good Master, what shall I do that I may inherit eternal life?"
> —*Matthew 10:17*

> And there are also many other things which Jesus did, the which, if they should be written every one, I suppose that even the world itself could not contain the books that should be written.
> —*John 21:25*

Maxwell Hillier

Copyright Maxwell Hillier © 2022
ISBN 9 781763 620728

Cover and title page inset painting:
Christ and the Rich Young Ruler by Heinrich Hofmann

Studies On The New Testament, Prof. F. Godet, D.D.
Hodder and Stoughton, 1873

Typeset in Minion Pro and Times 11/12
Scripture quotations in the *Authorized Version*

There Came One Running

The Hidden Story of the Rich Young Ruler

CONTENTS

Page	Foreword
1.	Mark's Account of The Rich Young Ruler
3.	1. The Rich Young Ruler
11.	2. The Eye of the Needle
19.	3. The Naked Man
27.	4. The Labourers
32.	5. The One Whom Jesus Loved
45.	6. Another Shall Gird You
51.	7. The Disciple Which Testified
58.	8. If I Will That He Tarry
65.	9. What Shall This Man Do?
73.	10. Testifying To These Things
80.	11. *Another* Disciple
94.	12. Another Revelation Of John
100.	13. Woman, Behold Your Son
110.	14. The *Other* Disciple
115.	15. Let Him Be as the Younger
122.	16. A Mask Removed

Supplementals:

124.	17. Mary Magdalene And Bethany
140.	18. Who Are My Brothers?
161.	19. Jesus Masters The Multitude
176.	20. One Come Late
192.	21. *Conclusion*

Foreword

This is the disciple which testifies of these things, and wrote these things: and we know that his testimony is true. And there are also many other things which Jesus did, the which, if they should be written every one, I suppose that even the world itself could not contain the books that should be written. Amen.
—*John 21:24-25*

THE APOSTLE JOHN, at the end of his gospel writes here of another gospel and in writing his gospel he is putting the finishing touches to his desire to recount many other things Jesus did, and inasmuch as many would be plain to see, some would be masked in subtleties. Here in this book we concern ourselves with some hidden stories in the New Testament that bear out the testimony of this apostle's statement.

The story of the rich young ruler is an intriguing one. It occurs in the gospels of Matthew, Mark and Luke. Who was this man? Why did he run to Christ? Did he follow him, and give away his riches? Or did he fall back into the crowd, shrouded and lost in his anonymity? Why does Mark not call him a *ruler* or a *young man*, as Luke and Matthew do? —and why does he say he came *running*, and that "Jesus beholding him loved him," while Matthew and Luke did not? Why did Jesus here say that "many who are first would be last and the last first?" The cover painting shows him unknown, his back toward us, a mystery. Do the gospel writers leave us ignorant on his destiny? In this book

FOREWORD

we will find answers to these questions, and in doing so we will challenge other long held assumptions.

We will use as our basis the story given in the gospel of Mark, the tenth chapter, and compare with the other gospels. Here we see the close relation of Mark with Peter, a relationship which will be borne out as we study further in this book. John's gospel was written last, and is supplemental to the others. He writes with them in mind, and it would be natural to observe how he complements them. He often removes details that have been expressed in the other gospels, for example, the baptism of Christ, where he simply says in chapter 1:32, "And John bare record, saying, I saw the Spirit descending from heaven like a dove, and it abode upon him," with no mention of what Matthew 3:14-17 had stated, in that he had submitted to baptism. In doing this John assumes an interdependence of the reader on the other gospel writers. We shall see that John has much more that is not explicitly stated, but nevertheless has much to show us for us to seek out.

In similar fashion lies a hidden story in the gospel accounts of Mary and the people of the house in Bethany, to which I append a chapter. I also make some observations in two chapters about Jesus' relatives in a study on Mark 1-3. Finally we examine some keys to the authorship of the Letter to the Hebrews.

I use the *Authorized Version* with some adjustments to the common English, as it has a poetic beauty that deserves to be cherished, that has not been surpassed.

Maxwell Hillier
November 2022

Mark's Account of The Rich Young Ruler

And when he was gone forth into the way, there came one running, and kneeled to him, and asked him, "Good Master, what shall I do that I may inherit eternal life?"

And Jesus said to him, "Why do you call me good? there is none good but one, that is, God. You know the commandments, Do not commit adultery, Do not kill, Do not steal, Do not bear false witness, Defraud not, Honour your father and mother.

And he answered and said to him, "Master, all these have I observed from my youth."

Then Jesus beholding him loved him, and said to him, One thing you lack: go your way, sell whatsoever you have, and give to the poor, and you shall have treasure in heaven: and come, take up the cross, and follow me.

And he was sad at that saying, and went away grieved: for he had great possessions.

And Jesus looked round about, and said to his disciples, How hardly shall they that have riches enter into the kingdom of God!

And the disciples were astonished at his words.

But Jesus answered again, and said to them, "Children, how hard is it for them that trust in riches to enter into the kingdom of God! It is easier for a camel to go through the eye of a needle, than for a rich man to enter into the kingdom of God."

And they were astonished out of measure, saying among themselves, "Who then can be saved?"

And Jesus looking upon them said, "With men it is impossible, but not with God: for with God all things are possible."

THERE CAME ONE RUNNING

Then Peter *began* to say to him, "Look, we have left all, and have followed you."

And Jesus answered and said, "Truly I say to you, There is no man that has left house, or brothers, or sisters, or father, or mother, or wife, or children, or lands, for my sake, and the gospel's, but he shall receive an hundredfold now in this time, houses, and brothers, and sisters, and mothers, and children, and lands, with persecutions; and in the world to come eternal life.
But many that are first shall be last; and the last first."

And they were in the way going up to Jerusalem; and Jesus went before them: and they were amazed; and as they followed, they were afraid.

And he took again the twelve, and began to tell them what things should happen unto him, saying, "Behold, we go up to Jerusalem; and the Son of man shall be delivered unto the chief priests, and unto the scribes; and they shall condemn him to death, and shall deliver him to the Gentiles: and they shall mock him, and shall scourge him, and shall spit upon him, and shall kill him: and the third day he shall rise again."

—*Mark 10:17-34*

1. The Rich Young Ruler

And he arose from there, and came into the coasts of Judaea by the farther side of Jordan: and the people resorted to him again; and, as he was accustomed, he taught them again. And the Pharisees came to him, and asked him, Is it lawful for a man to put away his wife? tempting him. And he answered and said to them, What did Moses command you? And they said, Moses suffered to write a bill of divorcement, and to put her away. And Jesus answered and said to them, For the hardness of your heart he wrote you this precept. But from the beginning of the creation God made them male and female. For this cause shall a man leave his father and mother, and cleave to his wife; And they two shall be one flesh: so then they are no more two, but one flesh. What therefore God has joined together, let not man put asunder. And in the house his disciples asked him again of the same matter. And he said to them, Whosoever shall put away his wife, and marry another, commits adultery against her. And if a woman shall put away her husband, and be married to another, she commits adultery. And they brought young children to him, that he should touch them: and his disciples rebuked those that brought them. But when Jesus saw it, he was much displeased, and said to them, Suffer the little children to come to me, and forbid them not: for of such is the kingdom of God. Truly I say unto you, Whosoever shall not receive the kingdom of God as a little child, he shall not enter therein. And he took them up in his arms, put his hands upon them, and blessed them.
—*Mark 10:1-16*

CHRIST HAD JUST entered into the region of Judea next to the Jordan, the very place in which a few years before he had been baptized by John the Baptist. Here the people flocked to him like

THERE CAME ONE RUNNING

sheep with a shepherd, hungry for his teaching. Into this holy resort, in the immediate events preceding the story of the young man in Mark chapter 10, in our text, the Pharisees, with malice, came to him with a question regarding divorce in order to ensnare him in his reply, that he might offend the rulers, who were far from obedience to the laws of marital fidelity, as Philip had the divorced Herodias to wife, and had killed John the Baptist for his withering judgment on his adultery. They hoped Jesus was to be snared into a similar trap, but he, deftly throwing them back upon their master, answered them with the question, "What did Moses command you?" Then he explained the holy union of marriage as intended from the creation in Genesis. He blessed the little children who had been brought to him, and showed the disciples that the kingdom of God is to be received as such. This scene forms a contrast to the hardhearted schemes of those who would lay aside the boundaries of the marriage union in unloving bills of divorcement. So it is that all this observes the crowd.

Then as the people had either dispersed or remained, Christ and his disciples had gone forth into the road to Jerusalem, and it was there that "there came one running," a young man, whom Luke calls a "rich young ruler," one of those "gorgeously apparelled who live in luxury in king's courts." This one would have been in the crowd, with his companions, perhaps he had come with the Pharisees, as a wealthy ruler he was known to them. Such social groups are held with cohesive bands, little islands of community in the crowd. This group was a pious group, as it appeared. He had observed the law, he and his friends appeared noble and outwardly

THE RICH YOUNG RULER

righteous, insofar as it concerned the performance of externals, in keeping with the expectations of a religious society which valued status and wealth. He had seen Jesus the Teacher defend the sanctity of marriage, and receive the little children to bless them despite the discouragement of his disciples, and this strikes a chord with him. Conscious of the group's hostility to Christ and their esteem of himself as a ruler, he waits until Jesus and the Pharisees and seekers had dispersed, and runs away from their view to seek Christ, and this he does in order to satisfy his hunger for eternal life, and so it is he comes running from the crowd alone to where Christ and his disciples had come on the way to Jerusalem. Here we have this one, nurtured in the ways and the laws of this society, a young man, a ruler, who has observed the commandments from his youth, who has kept the law, is possessed of chattels, status, land and property, an inheritance, a promising future, a man who possesses *everything*, yet he still lacks *one* thing, and that is the thing he asks for—on his knees, "Good master, what shall I do that I may inherit *eternal life*?"

A few years prior near this very place on the Jordan the fishermen among the disciples had come to Christ as they followed John the Baptist. They were a group of young men from the north, free of the pressure of the politics of the religious leaders in the south, not part of a group hostile to the Lord, but ones who shared the common bonds of brotherhood as they entered into the circle of the disciples of Jesus. They were well aware their northern homeland was to see the light according to ancient prophecy, as Isaiah 9:1-2 had spoken, "Nevertheless the dimness shall not be such as was in her vexation, when at the first he lightly afflicted the land of Zebulun and the land of Naphtali, and afterward did more grievously afflict her by the way of the sea, beyond Jordan, in Galilee of the nations. The people that walked in darkness have seen a great light: they that dwell in the land of the shadow of death, upon them has the light shined." But this young man was of the religious families of the holy city, he had followed the law diligently from his youth, and this among his young colleagues. He was a *young ruler*, with a position in the Jerusalem community, he had inherited great wealth, he was a man with a future, holding status and friendship with the leaders of the nation. Yet this was a man who hungered for something more, one whom the Lord had set his love upon, as the gospel writer says, "Jesus beholding him loved him."

Now Jesus is no mere man, behind the veil of flesh he is the LORD, the Almighty, the Son of God the Father, One filled with the Holy Spirit without measure, the Maker of heaven and earth, of all things seen and unseen. In the gospels, when he acts and speaks, so also the Father and the Holy Spirit is at work. The Lord our God is indeed one Lord. Christ is all and in all. He is enthroned above the cherubim, all creatures are subject to him. Even the wind and the seas obey him, in him all things are working together. Luther said "when God speaks it understands a word related to a real thing or action, not just a sound as ours is. When the sun rises and sets, when the fruits grow, when human beings are born, God speaks. His words are not empty air, but things very great and wonderful, which we see with our eyes and feel with our hands. When he said let there be

THE RICH YOUNG RULER

a sun, a moon, let the earth bring forth trees, as soon as he said it, it was done." Christ's words to this young man, then, are not to be regarded as simple sounds at play in the air as if spoken by a mere man. When we look at this story we can assume that more is at work, that there is more to come, even if it be hid from us, which in fact, as we will demonstrate, it is.

As the Pharisees had a question posed to them, "What did Moses command you?" so here also a question is posed to the young man, who had asked, "Good Master, what shall I do that I may inherit eternal life?" The question, which at heart, is really the answer to the man's question was, "And Jesus said unto him, 'Why do you call Me good? There is none good but one, that is, God.' " The answer to the inheriting the eternal life is thus found in faith, in believing, in the acknowledgment of who Christ is, that he is in fact the Son of God, it is the acknowledgement of the Father and the Son. At the first, in the fulfilment of prophecy, in the showing of the Messiah to Israel, we see it as John the Baptist had once said in that very locale, on the Jordan, in the first chapter of John's gospel:

> And I knew him not: but he that sent me to baptize with water, the same said to me, Upon whom you shall see the Spirit descending, and remaining on him, the same is he which baptizes with the Holy Ghost. And I saw, and bare record that this is the Son of God. Again the next day after John stood, and two of his disciples; And looking upon Jesus as he walked, he said, Behold the Lamb of God!

And the apostle later declares in his epistle,

> That which was from the beginning, which we have heard, which we have seen with our eyes, which we have looked

upon, and our hands have handled, of the Word of life;
(For the life was manifested, and we have seen it, and bear
witness, and show unto you that eternal life, which was
with the Father, and was manifested unto us;) That which
we have seen and heard declare we unto you, that you also
may have fellowship with us: and truly our fellowship is
with the Father, and with his Son Jesus Christ. And these
things write we unto you, that your joy may be full.

Whosoever shall confess that Jesus is the Son of God,
God dwells in him, and he in God.

Who is he that overcomes the world,
but he that believes that Jesus is the Son of God?

The fellowship is with the Father and the Son. We also see it in the Lord's Prayer—"Our Father which art in heaven, hallowed be thy name." We say not "who" but "which" indicating a compound, that is the name to which we are immersed in baptism, the name of the Father is "the Father *and* the Son *and* the Holy Spirit." God is one. Thus we say that the Son and the Spirit is divine or holy, even as 1 John 4:15 reads, "Whosoever shall confess that Jesus is the Son of God, God dwells in him, and he in God." There in the prayer in the hallowing our confession of faith resides.

The young man sought eternal life, and here it is found in the person of Christ. The young man had addressed Jesus as "Good Master," that is "Good Rabbi" or "Teacher," —he had as yet no conception of who Jesus really was. He was hardly far from being a child himself, and he had only just seen Jesus declare, "Suffer the little children to come unto me, and forbid them not: for of such is the kingdom of God." In heart he would still feel as a child, his awkward manhood

THE RICH YOUNG RULER

barely formed. The disciples had discouraged the children from being led to the master, but he had seen the master receive them. The lad comes to Christ despite the followers. Here, so close to the Jordan and the place where John had come heralding the Messiah, where the disciples had come to believe the Lord a few years before, as Christ makes his way to Jerusalem to be killed, we have this young man being introduced to the Son of God with the words, "There is none good but one, that is, God." In this phrase the divine logic and implication is thus offered to this man:

*You call me good—Jesus is good—God is good—
Only God is good = Then Jesus must be God.*

It is the word of Moses, the "hear" of "Hear, O Israel, the Lord our God is one Lord" presented to this man. There the "one Lord" is declared, not to show one person of God, but to show the unity of the Trinity. It is the fellowship of the mystery, of the Father and the Son, hid from the beginning of time. Colossians 2:2 reads, "That their hearts might be comforted, being knit together in love, and unto all riches of the full assurance of understanding, to the acknowledgement of the mystery of God, and of the Father, and of Christ." Here is shown the eternal life, manifested to him and to us for fellowship, that our joy may be full.

But the lad here goes away sorrowful, for he has many possessions. We should not make the mistake of considering the man as hard-hearted and uninterested, he is sorrowful because he is also zealously desirous of Christ. It is not a casual interest, he comes *running*.

Christ had said in Luke 16:16, "The law and the prophets were until John: since that time the kingdom of God is preached, and every man *presses* into it." If the young man had no interest he would not be sad. One thing is for sure he would have had friends, as the rich often attract opportunists. In telling him to sell what he has and give to the poor Jesus is disengaging him from harmful relationships, from community ties and bonds antithetical to the kingdom of Christ.

Now at this point Jesus plies the lad with his statement regarding certain commandments, to which the young man says ingenuously that he has observed since his youth. Here is a lad that has a genuine desire for goodness, as Mark 10:21 shows:

> Then Jesus beholding him loved him, and said to him, "One thing you lack: go your way, sell whatsoever you have, and give to the poor, and you shall have treasure in heaven: and come, take up the cross, and follow me."

The man goes away, in fact Christ has told him to go away, and to sell his possessions, give away the money to the poor, and then to take up the cross and follow him to the death. Jesus had not asked this of Peter or of James and John. Although Peter had said "We have left all and followed you!" he still had his nets and his father to go back to. There were rich women in Jesus' band, with a wealthy purse. Judas held the bag. This is not a requirement of all and sundry, but it was Jesus' request of this particular young man. However, the man goes away sad as he has many possessions. And traditionally this is where the church has always left him. The record seems silent on his fate, but is it?

2. The Eye of the Needle

And Jesus looked round about, and said to his disciples, How hardly shall they that have riches enter into the kingdom of God! And the disciples were astonished at his words. But Jesus answered again, and said to them, Children, how hard is it for them that trust in riches to enter into the kingdom of God! It is easier for a camel to go through the eye of a needle, than for a rich man to enter into the kingdom of God.
—*Mark 10:23*

Now Jesus addresses his disciples on the difficulty of entering the kingdom with riches. In *Aramaic*, the language Jesus was speaking, the word "camel," is spelled the same as "rope"— "gml." They sound different, but written Aramaic does not often represent vowels. In the Koine Greek "camel" / *kamelon* and "rope" are also the same word, distinguished textually by a single vowel yet pronounced almost the same. Considered as a *camel* the intention of the verse is still the same, the difficulty and absurdity of the exercise. Considered as a *rope* however we can draw some other inferences. To put a rope through the eye of a needle one must unravel and discard many of the threads to but one. Thus this rich young man needed to divest himself of his riches, his "threads" to go through the eye of the needle. Here stands a signal warning to greedy Judas, who would fail to enter into the kingdom of God, rich with his thirty pieces he is unable to thread the needle, gripping his "rope" he would soon hang himself.

These words of the Messiah were a source of

astonishment to the disciples. They must have held the belief their being with Christ would bring them wealth along with power. But Jesus repeats, "How hard is it for them that trust in riches to enter into the kingdom of God!" The disciples are amazed at this teaching, astonished out of measure, wondering who then can be saved. Perhaps it was the tipping point for greedy Judas. Peter responds and *begins* to say, perhaps afraid for his salvation, or boastfully in comparison to new disciples, to reaffirm his position in the kingdom pecking order, "Look, we have left all and followed you—," but Christ overrides him assuring reward for *all* those who have left house, family or lands for his sake and the gospel's as verse 23 reads:

Then Peter began to say to him, Look, we have left all, and have followed you. And Jesus answered and said, Truly I say to you, There is no man that has left house, or brothers, or sisters, or father, or mother, or wife, or children, or lands, for my sake, and the gospel's, but he shall receive an hundredfold now in this time, houses, and brothers, and sisters, and mothers, and children, and lands, with persecutions; and in the world to come eternal life. But many that are first shall be last; and the last first.

Note well, other wives are not promised to those who leave their wife for the gospel's sake, instead persecutions! Now Peter is cut off by Jesus, as it is said he *began to say*, he is not permitted to complete his utterance here as Jesus discourses on the benefits of forsaking house and family for Christ and the gospel. They are not suffered to boast upon their reputation and actions as the basis for being worthy of the kingdom. Jesus says, "no man," the reference is not merely for the twelve, but all potential disciples are included. Up

THE EYE OF THE NEEDLE

to the last statement the disciples may have thought all well and good, but then Jesus concludes with the troubling enigmatic phrase, "But many that are first shall be last; and the last first." What could be meant? "We have left all and followed him, thrown away our nets," thinks Peter, as if to say, "We have been with him from the beginning—are the last to join have greater privileges?" This must have cut off the ambitious air of the disciples, the possibility that they who were first might be last. The parable of the labourers, which he would soon subsequently teach them, speaks to this.

Now all this is taught in the context of the calling of the rich young man. Jesus is calling someone to his band late in the story, into a cohesive and privileged group who had been there some time, even a few years. The disciples' keenness and ambition for position in Christ's kingdom is displayed in verse 37, where James and John request: "Grant unto us that we may sit, one on your right hand, and the other on your left hand, in your glory." But Christ's word leaves the disciples astonished, fearful of their salvation, this together with the uncertainty of persecutions promised to them:

> And they were astonished out of measure, saying among themselves, "Who then can be saved?" And Jesus looking upon them said, "With men it is impossible, but not with God: for with God all things are possible."

And verse 32 adds, "And they were in the way going up to Jerusalem; and Jesus went before them: and they were amazed; and as they followed, they were afraid."

The little band follow Christ to Jerusalem with no arms, no wealth, only the power of His person and word. Jesus, the long promised Messiah, would illustrate this by arriving, not with the powerful trappings of warhorse, arms and soldiers, but in the poverty of riding on a colt the foal of an ass, as foretold by the prophet Zechariah, and accompanied with humble fishermen. In the calling of the rich young ruler Christ displays a kingdom independent of riches. In this final Passover journey to Jerusalem Jesus would come in a circuit from the wilderness of Ephraim to Jericho, gathering in the pilgrims along the route, where he would call little Zacchaeus down from his tree, and stay with him the night, who in gratitude would pay back his extortions and give to the poor. Matthew, or Levi the son of Alphaeus had left it to Mark to recount his own conversion. He no doubt was wealthy, but he did not have the trappings of religious status to hold him back from following Christ as the rich young ruler had, tax collectors being scorned by the religious, yet as proved by Levi's celebration, Mark 2:14, loved by sinners.

Jesus had declared regarding the wealthy, "With men it is impossible, but not with God, for with God all things are possible." He is showing his disciples that *it is possible* for a wealthy man, even the young man, to enter the kingdom, to thread the needle. This declaration along with the question to the young man, "Why do you call me good? there is none good but one, that is, God," displays two statements about God— namely that His will is irresistible, and that Jesus is very God. Here Christ is showing that the young man has a way through, to follow along with the others. Here you are not dealing with a mere rabbi, but the Son of God, believe this—that Christ is God, then you are with God, whom to know is everlasting life. It is a lot to take in, the young man has gone away sad and grieved, he has much to think about. "Why do you call me good?" must have been echoing around his mind for days. The answer to this question could potentially lead him to eternal life. He goes away sad as if there were no hope for him, but Christ assures his disciples all things are possible.

He had presented the young man with commands he knew he could truly say, "I have kept." Honest and faithful in his reply he shows no hypocrisy. It is here that it is tenderly said, "Then Jesus beholding him loved him." Such love was perhaps undergirded by the young man's witness of the reception of the children by Jesus, despite their discouragement in Mark 10:13-14:

> And they brought young children to him, that he should touch them: and his disciples rebuked those that brought them. But when Jesus saw it, he was much displeased, and said to them, Suffer the little children to come unto me, and forbid them not: for of such is the kingdom of God.

The inner circle would prove no barrier to the man as the shepherd had presented an open door. Here in this account in this gospel it seems the words of someone who has experienced it. Such love in a look is a thing best known to the recipient. That look was not confined to him, others would have experienced it, but here it stands out in the narrative and why? Surely because it was the experience of someone known to the gospel writer, and it was also the driving power in the extraordinary conversion and calling of the man, whom Christ had laid a heavy demand to give away all he had. Mark could not have known the feeling of love given to the man unless the man had let him know. If the rich man lost in his gold and status would not be seen again, how could Mark know of this personal beholding the man experienced? He was particularly defined amongst others by this love of Christ toward him. Why would it be written thus unless the gospel writer knew the recipient of Christ's loving beholding?

It is then that Christ tells him that he lacks one thing. This is someone who in the common course of life has everything—family, piety, land, inheritance, position, power, friends and colleagues, a bright future. That one thing is to sell and give away everything he has to the poor, and the invitation is, "Come, take up the cross and follow me." Such a paradox Christ throws at him! One thing you lack, and that is to give away everything and go with Jesus to the death! —he has come to Christ for eternal *life*! He wants to escape death yet he is given a death, the one thing he knows he has! This command struck at the heart of the man like lightning.

One command that Christ had not mentioned, "You shall not covet," came at the young man under the request of Christ that he give away all he has, much like Paul's dilemma in Romans 7:7, "for I had not known lust (desire) except the law had said, You shall not covet." Paul would also say he died a death, "But sin, taking occasion by the commandment, wrought in me all manner of concupiscence. For without the law sin was dead. For I was alive without the law once: but when the commandment came, sin revived, and I died. And the commandment, which was ordained to life, I found to be unto death." To the young man the other command unmentioned was the first, "You shall have no other gods before me," that is, fidelity to the worship

THE EYE OF THE NEEDLE

of the one true God, and it was this command that was addressed in Jesus' question, "Why do you call me good? there is none good but God."

The man had asked, "What *must I do* to inherit eternal life?" Our deeds, personality and sanctity, what we *do*, do not merit us eternal life—but the deeper state of our heart, that which constitutes our *belief* does—the faith in the one true God and his Son. This command to sell and give all away forced the man to acknowledge his sinfulness, his peccadillo, such a typically *Jewish* one—his sin of covetousness, which had clothed his whole life with position, status, power, wealth, friends and family—to acknowledge this was a necessary admission to him in order to receive the mercy of God. Jesus does not merely present the law to him, here Jesus does ask him to *do* something, and that is, to give it all away! And it strikes across his life like a death. Indeed Christ asks him to take up the cross *with him*. He does not say *your* cross but *the* cross. Here is not a general plea to self-denial, as we often take it, but it is an invitation to follow Christ himself to the death of *the* very cross itself in Jerusalem. This is the story as it unfolds. This is how the young man would have understood it.

Together with this it is the love of Christ that struck this young man also, "Jesus beholding him loved him," and it is this love that can only enable such a one to fulfil such a demand as Christ gives him. Such a "beholding" invites a respondent beholding, and this is described by Paul in 2 Corinthians 3:15:

But even unto this day, when Moses is read, the vail is upon their heart. Nevertheless when it shall turn to the Lord, the vail shall be taken away. Now the Lord is that Spirit: and where the Spirit of the Lord is, there is liberty. But we all, with open face beholding as in a glass the glory of the Lord, are changed into the same image from glory to glory, even as by the Spirit of the Lord.

Moses is read to a man, the law comes at him accusing him, but this man's heart, that of the rich young ruler, is turned to the Lord, here *bodily* before him, he beholds his very person, the vail is taken away in the gospel. In Jesus he sees God, the Father. In this beholding of Jesus was a display of the glory of the Lord. Such a beholding is not static, but transforming, we are changed into the same image, even to the death of the cross. Here in this love is true liberty and freedom. It remains to be seen then, whether the young man would take up the offer, as he goes away. Yet although Christ had said "Go your way, etc.," —the going did not represent a denial, as he had also said, "And *come*..."

Now afterward, to the twelve, Christ explained in detail what awaited him, what was meant by "taking up the cross," Mark 10:33-34:

> Saying, Behold, we go up to Jerusalem; and the Son of man shall be delivered to the chief priests, and to the scribes; and they shall condemn him to death, and shall deliver him to the Gentiles: and they shall mock him, and shall scourge him, and shall spit upon him, and shall kill him: and the third day he shall rise again.

To this they were amazed and afraid. To this Christ had invited the young man to bear witness. It remained to be seen whether this man would thread the needle and go with Christ to his death on the cross.

3. The Naked Man

And immediately, while he yet spake, comes Judas, one of the twelve, and with him a great multitude with swords and staves, from the chief priests and the scribes and the elders. And he that betrayed him had given them a token, saying, "Whomsoever I shall kiss, that same is he; take him, and lead him away safely." And as soon as he was come, he goes straightway to him, and says, "Master, master;" and kissed him. And they laid their hands on him, and took him. And one of them that stood by drew a sword, and smote a servant of the high priest, and cut off his ear. And Jesus answered and said to them, "Are you come out, as against a thief, with swords and with staves to take me? I was daily with you in the temple teaching, and you took me not: but the scriptures must be fulfilled." And they all forsook him, and fled. And there followed him a certain young man, having a linen cloth cast about his naked body; and the young men laid hold on him: And he left the linen cloth, and fled from them naked.
—*Mark 14:43-52*

Now when Christ was betrayed we have the curious account in Mark chapter 14 of the "certain young man," who courageously followed a little after everyone else had fled the betrayal. The phrase "immediately while he yet spake *comes* Judas, one of the twelve," reads in the present tense like the language of an eye-witness, one etched in his memory, when Judas comes to "take Christ and lead him away." The phrase "one of them that stood by draws a sword," is a self-effacing of Peter who had bravely acted with it, as John reveals in his gospel, chapter 18:10, posthumous to Peter's death, that it was in fact Peter with the sword.

THERE CAME ONE RUNNING

Now Mark's "certain young man" of verses 51-52 seems a superfluous addition to the account of the betrayal, but if we consider it in relation to the "rich young man" of chapter 10 we can make some inferences and conclusions, and a hidden story emerges. This information has context. Mark's gospel is filled with urgent *hurry*, many *immediatelys* and *straightways* carrying us along between each episode. Is this man the one come running, the rich young man with many possessions? He comes *running* into the gospel, a man in a hurry. Here in chapter 14 this *certain young man* seems bereft of possessions, having only a mere linen cloth cast about his naked body. While following Christ he is beset by other young men who seek to lay hold of him, and he in a final act leaves the linen cloth and flees from the young men stark naked. He comes in hurry, and leaves in flight. Consider Jesus' request of the rich young man here, Mark 10:21:

> Then Jesus beholding him loved him, and said to him, One thing you lack: go your way, sell whatsoever you have, and give to the poor, and you shall have treasure in heaven: and come, take up the cross, and follow me.

The young man, as Luke 7:25 says, one "gorgeously apparelled and living in king's courts," is told to follow Jesus and take up the cross, to sell and give away to the poor *whatsoever* he has, which includes of course his rich clothing, his gorgeous apparel, and here in Gethsemane we are faced with a young man following Christ to the cross with only a linen cloth cast about his naked body. He is bereft of wealthy clothing apart from the modesty of linen cloth. Linen belonged to the wealthy. He is a "certain" young man, a man who

THE NAKED MAN

has reference to our knowledge of the story in some particular way—"certain" indicates someone of whom must bear some particulars available to our knowledge, even such as Mark has shown us in the young ruler. He is a "young" man, and it is "young men" who lay hold on him. As Judas and his men lay hold of Christ, these young men lay hold of this young man. This young man then has allied himself to Christ, and is being arrested by his colleagues who are juniors allied to the chief priests, scribes and elders. The young man who came running from the crowd near the Jordan in all likelihood had run from his *peers, young men,* to Christ. That they attempted to arrest him shows us that he had already allied himself with Christ and the disciples. It remains to be seen at what point he had allied himself.

The account of the naked man makes little sense, unless it be a personal account, known to the author, that is, Mark, who wished to include it, but in a way that was discreet and did not draw undue attention, as if a matter of pride, or abashed at the man's shame in nakedness, or in sensitivity to his family's reputation in the community, or most likely a desire not to clutter or detract from the narrative of Christ's death. It is as if it needs be recorded yet with great delicacy, brevity, subtlety and tact, much like as John would write regarding the identity of Mary and Martha's husband— namely the severe Simon the leper in Bethany, as we will see in the chapter on Mary's household. The gospel would go out into a broad readership, and would have to observe certain sensibilities to folk living, involved with the narrative.

That the young man was a rich ruler was later told

by Luke, but not defined so exactly as Mark, with whom it is simply "a young man." Mark chose here not to call him a *rich* man. After all, here is a man who had now given it all away. The naked man at the betrayal is a *certain* young man, a particular person who would be known to us. It does seem apt to consider it as the rich young man, as with it we see a striking fulfilment of the word of Christ to that man to give away all he had, and with this to follow Christ, to take up his cross, to the very end, even to the loss of all his *clothing*, as Christ had commanded him. One cannot think of another reason why it would be included in the account. It must be there because it has an import of some kind. The gospel writers are not given to unnecessary superfluities. Every word has weight and import. Mark is giving us information, to be sought out by those who seek. Here we have a man called to take up the cross of Christ, to follow him to the death, to witness the death of Christ. This would include the betrayal in Gethsemene.

The account of the betrayal would be the word of one who observed it at first hand, an eye-witness, it therefore has an *immediacy*, to use a favourite word of Mark. It certainly has that feel to it, verse 43, "And *immediately* while he yet spake, comes Judas," being recounted in the present tense, as one does regarding first hand occurrences. Judas was not just a man now, but the personification of the devil himself, when the gospel writer sees him come to Gethsemane, he sees a fearsome creature in all his darkness, of whom the others are unaware, and this is something the young man is particularly defined as knowing, as will be presently seen. It is likely then that the man was also witness to what preceded, that is, the tiredness of the disciples and the prayer of Christ as recounted in Luke. Those lacking clothes struggle to sleep. If he would witness this death then it is to the end that he would bear testimony to it. This young man then must be Mark himself. *Mark was the rich young ruler.*

Godet observes, "Mark's gospel bears the character of personal witness, with vivid local colouring and directly personal recollection with its graphic touches, see 4:38, 10:50, 6:31, 7:34 and moral impressions also, see 3:5, 10:21, 32, catching fleeting expressions of anger or of love in Christ and secret emotions of the disciples at important moments. He preserves the Aramaic expressions while translating them into Greek, as if he still heard the sound of Jesus' voice." Jesus had promised the young man treasure in heaven, "treasure" is *thesaurus*, as in *Roget's Thesaurus* of synonyms. It is a casket, a store of precious things. The gospels are as synonyms that sparkle with each other. In Matthew 13, we read that "every scribe which is instructed unto the kingdom of heaven is like unto a man that is an householder, which brings forth out of *his treasure* things new and old." In the gospel of Mark we find embodied that very thing, a storehouse of heavenly treasure, some of it hidden and buried.

We know that Mark was a companion of *Peter*, who had denied Christ at the cock-calling yet who found gentle and loving restoration by the risen Christ. Here it seems Mark was a companion with him in the very events of the Passion. In his first epistle Peter calls Mark his *son*: "The church that is at Babylon, elected together with you, salutes you; and so does Marcus my son." In John 21 Christ had told Peter to "feed his little ones," and here in the epistle we see that he has taken Mark under his wing, here in its Latin form of *Marcus*.

Such a one as a young ruler would be a lettered person, educated, given the privilege of being able to write as a scribe to the things he has heard and witnessed, appropriate to a Mark the gospel writer, in the company of a Peter, an unlettered Galilean fisherman. It is fitting that he be a fellow witness to the sufferings and resurrection of Christ, and that "the one whom Jesus beholding loved" should find such a place in the kingdom of God. Peter discusses with Jesus in Mark 10:

> Then Peter began to say to him, Look, we have left all, and have followed you. And Jesus answered and said, Truly I say to you, There is no man that has left house, or brothers, or sisters, or father, or mother, or wife, or children, or lands, for my sake, and the gospel's, but he shall receive an hundredfold now in this time, houses, and brothers, and sisters, and mothers, and children, and lands, with persecutions; and in the world to come eternal life. But many that are first shall be last; and the last first.

If these relations are as we suggest, then these words take on a greater circumference. The young man, Mark, has joined the circle of Peter, those who have left all to follow Christ—"Lo, we have left all and followed you." He has "left house, brothers and family, and lands for Christ's sake and the gospel's." Indeed he has *written* a gospel, he then is promised a hundredfold now in this time, *houses* and *brothers* and sisters, mothers, children, lands, persecutions, and in the world to come, eternal life, of which the young man was searching. We will also see he is given a mother and a house. And here, in fulfilment of the promise, in Peter's epistolary salutation,

THE NAKED MAN

"The church that is at Babylon, elected together with you, salutes you; and so doth Marcus my son," here he is in the apostle's epistle, in another land—Italy, with Peter, a prince among the apostles, at the very heart of the world power, its Babylon, *Rome*, saluting his readers. We see his name at the end of the letter to Philemon written by Paul from Rome, among all the *brothers* of Paul: verses 23-24, "There salute you Epaphras, my fellow prisoner in Christ Jesus; *Marcus*, Aristarchus, Demas, Lucas, my fellow labourers." Here he is with the other gospel writer, or secretary of Paul, that is Lucas, or Luke. Also we have Demas, who forsook Paul, "having loved this present world," 2 Timothy 4:10, a weakness for which Mark had been cured, a love that had been eclipsed by a brighter love.

Here the rope in the eye of the needle has connections. John writes of Christ's robe in chapter 19:23-24,

> Then the soldiers, when they had crucified Jesus, took his garments, and made four parts, to every soldier a part; and also his coat: now the coat was without seam, woven from the top throughout. They said therefore among themselves, Let us not rend it, but cast lots for it, whose it shall be: that the scripture might be fulfilled, which said, They parted my raiment among them, and for my vesture they did cast lots.

The robe was of a single thread. And here the certain young man loses all his clothing, all his *threads*. He gives away all he has. Here Jesus declares that "many that are first are last, and the last first." The one of whom it was said, "how hardly they that have riches shall enter into the kingdom of God," enters in and takes up the cross—the very death of Christ; and the rope that was to go through this eye of the needle goes through as a slender thread, he has cast off his old life with its familial relations and friendships and entered into a new one with its new houses, brothers, sisters, lands and eternal life. The rope has shed its extra threads to go through the eye of the needle as a naked strand, the young man has literally cast off every single thread and garment, in giving away all he had. Christ was parted from his robe, crucified naked to his cross, and this young man loses all his clothes. He is no longer the rich man. Here we have a disciple of Christ in the same vein as the repentant thief on his cross, or Simon of Cyrene who was compelled to bear Christ's cross— it is as Jesus said, "My Father works hitherto, and I work." As Christ calls the thief as he is dying, he has also called this young man on the way to his death to be with him at his betrayal, he recruits a herald who would proclaim his words and his death to the world; there is a marvellous casual effortlessness at work in this calling. On the road to Jerusalem to the cross Christ tells one come running to take up the cross, and so it is we have a disciple come late, one that is last. As we will see in the next chapter the many that are first are last— Peter and they who fled at the arrest of Christ, yet this certain young man follows even further, taking up the cross, to the loss of all he has, even the linen cloth—and so the last becomes the first.

Judas however holds the bag, loves his riches: he desires to take Christ and lead him away to judgment, turning his master into silver, the price of blood, and later as Satan casts him aside, he is left to his hopeless remorse, when the judgment turns upon him, he is driven to suicide—he takes a rope and strangles himself.

4. The Labourers

For the kingdom of heaven is like unto a man that is an householder, which went out early in the morning to hire labourers into his vineyard. And when he had agreed with the labourers for a penny a day, he sent them into his vineyard. And he went out about the third hour, and saw others standing idle in the marketplace, And said unto them; "Go you also into the vineyard, and whatsoever is right I will give you." And they went their way. Again he went out about the sixth and ninth hour, and did likewise. And about the eleventh hour he went out, and found others standing idle, and said unto them, "Why do you stand here all the day idle?" They say unto him, "Because no man has hired us." He said unto them, "Go you also into the vineyard; and whatsoever is right, that shall you receive". So when even was come, the lord of the vineyard said unto his steward, "Call the labourers, and give them their hire, beginning from the last unto the first." And when they came that were hired about the eleventh hour, they received every man a penny. But when the first came, they supposed that they should have received more; and they likewise received every man a penny. And when they had received it, they murmured against the goodman of the house, saying, "These last have wrought but one hour, and you have made them equal unto us, which have borne the burden and heat of the day." But he answered one of them, and said, "Friend, I do you no wrong: did not you agree with me for a penny? Take that is yours, and go your way: I will give unto this last, even as unto you. Is it not lawful for me to do what I will with mine own? Is your eye evil, because I am good?" So the last shall be first, and the first last: for many be called, but few chosen.

—*Matthew 20:1-16*

THERE CAME ONE RUNNING

Now Matthew's account of the rich young man, chapter 19:16-30, is associated with this *immediately ensuing* parable of the labourers in his gospel, chapter 20:1-16, which was placed *just before* the account of the going up to Jerusalem and the informing the disciples of his death, 20:17-19. The narrative arrangement concerns the calling of the rich young ruler, the relations of the parable of the labourers, some called early and some late, with the owner of the vineyard, being illustrated in the surrounding events with which it is connected, that is, Christ and his close relationships with the disciples. This parable, in its context here has an immediate bearing on the events surrounding Christ with its relation with the different players, that is, the rich young man and the twelve disciples, and its psychological implications. We must always observe first the relation of parable to the gospel stories and characters to which they are embodied before making application to our own context.

In the parable labourers are called "early in the morning." In John 1:37-45 Peter, James, John, Andrew, Nathanael and Philip first came to follow Christ, having been followers of John the Baptist. "About the third hour, the sixth and the ninth, *others* were standing idle in the *market place*." —in Mark 2:13-14 Matthew is called to follow Christ near the sea side of Capernaum at the receipt of custom, that is, at the market. Now with this young man Christ enlists a labourer at the eleventh hour, "Go you also into the vineyard, and whatsoever is right that shall you receive." When the evening was come and time for a payment, those that received first were those he hired last. Those who had wrought but one

THE LABOURERS

hour he had made equal with those who had borne the burden and heat of the whole day, all receiving a penny. Jesus concludes with the word, "So the last shall be first, and the first last: for many be called, but few chosen." Now Peter, one called early, says "Look, we have left all and followed you . . ." but is cut off with Christ's words, "There is no man who has left house, or brothers, etc." — where we have the same concluding words in verse 31: "But many that are first shall be last; and the last first." Thus Christ has immediately applied the parable to Peter and the disciples. This common phrase then suggests a common theme, which is that of *the labourers*. This theme relates to the apostles and disciples of Christ, and it is said in the first instance for *their* benefit and instruction in light of their relationship with Christ. Consider these words from the parable in verse 13,

> But he answered one of them, and said, Friend, I do you no wrong: did not you agree with me for a penny? Take what is yours, and go your way: I will give unto this last, even as unto you. Is it not lawful for me to do what I will with my own? Is your eye evil, because I am good?

These could all be applied to Peter and the disciples, *and* the young man. "I will give unto this last even as unto you," — Mark and Peter would *share* the honour of Mark's gospel. Matthew, the tax collector, one also called later than the first, despite the odium of his profession, would receive a similar honour. In this light these words are remarkably prophetic and prescient.

Here in the parable Christ is addressing the relations among the disciples, how they feel about *newcomers*; it refers to brotherly love. Christ gives the new ones the same privileges and rewards, the older ones feel jealous and defensive, and accuse the owner of the vineyard of unfairness.

And here compare a word regarding the Good Teacher and his goodness, in the calling of the rich young ruler, "Why do you call me good? there is none good but God," with, "Is your eye evil because I am *good*?" The goodness relates to his unmeasured generosity. And compare the phrase, "With God all things are possible," in regard to the young ruler with this parable, "and is it not lawful for me to do what I will with mine own?" This theme of doing what I will, and "take that is yours and go your way" relates to Peter and the young man if we would consider further what follows. It is a primary axiom that one can do what one wants with one's own. That others are given the same for less labour does not imply unfairness on the owner of the vineyard, but this accusation of unfairness is the "evil eye," the problem is with the workers, not the owner— "Whatsoever is right that shall you receive, did you not agree for a penny?" The owner is good, but the complainants have an evil eye. "*Good* master," said the rich young ruler, to which Christ had said, "Why do you call me good? There is none good but God." The young man had confessed the goodness of the Master, and in that goodness was invited to find from where that goodness had sprung. The disciples, who had been with him much longer, however, are warned, they are in danger of denying that goodness with an evil eye.

The parable had regard to the love of money, and the offence caused in relation with the dispensation of it. This warning was in dead earnest, for as it turned

THE LABOURERS

out, that is what happened with one of them, Judas the son of Simon, who loved the purse, would betray his master for thirty pieces of silver. And it was this love of money and possessions that was the stumbling block to the young man, as Mark writes, "he was sad at that saying, and went away grieved: for he had great possessions."

This one then is not admitted to the work in the vineyard immediately, he must await the coming of the householder. The last that had wrought "but one hour" had been made equal to those who had borne the burden and heat of the whole day. In Luke 22:53 Jesus said to those who came to arrest him,"When I was with you daily in the temple, you did not try to seize Me. But this is your *hour*, and the power of darkness." This hour then was the time of the young man's labour, in a bearing witness to Christ's death even as Mark 12:7-8 details the parable of the vineyard, "But those husbandmen said among themselves, This is the heir; come, let us kill him, and the inheritance shall be ours. And they took him, and killed him, and cast him out of the vineyard."

5. The One Whom Jesus Loved

When Jesus had thus said, he was troubled in spirit, and testified, and said, "Truly, truly, I say unto you, that one of you shall betray me." Then the disciples looked one on another, doubting of whom he spoke. Now there was leaning on Jesus' bosom one of his disciples, whom Jesus loved. Simon Peter therefore beckoned to him, that he should ask who it should be of whom he spoke. He then lying on Jesus' breast says unto him, "Lord, who is it?" Jesus answered, "He it is, to whom I shall give a sop, when I have dipped it." And when he had dipped the sop, he gave it to Judas Iscariot, the son of Simon.
—*John 13:21-26*

HERE IN THE thirteenth chapter of John's gospel we read of the one "whom Jesus loved" leaning on Jesus' bosom at the Passover. Peter asks this one to let him know who was the betrayer, then that one asks Jesus, "Lord who is it?" Now in John 21:20, *after* the events of the cross and the resurrection, Peter is with Jesus on the beach, after the miraculous draught of fishes, and he turns about to see, as it is put, the disciple "whom Jesus loved" following. Now we have always assumed that this one is the apostle *John*, that John is referring obliquely to himself, yet in the story of the young man, we have the same appellation, "then Jesus beholding him loved him." The young man on his bosom at the Passover is named "the one whom Jesus loved." Is he the one whom "Jesus beholding him loved

THE ONE WHOM JESUS LOVED

him?"—the rich young ruler? Could this be his nickname? If this is so, then the young man is not John but rather the young man with many possessions who had thus entered into his discipleship before the Passover, as he was with Christ *there*, in that large upper room, addressing Jesus as Lord—"*Lord,* who is it?"

We read of the later scene on the beach thus in 21:1:

> After these things Jesus showed himself again to the disciples at the sea of Tiberias; and on this wise showed he himself. There were together Simon Peter, and Thomas called Didymus, and Nathanael of Cana in Galilee, and the sons of Zebedee, and two other of his disciples.

There was "Simon Peter, and the sons of Zebedee," that is James and John, and there were "two other of his disciples." These two disciples were not necessarily of the apostles, as they would have been called by name, as the others were, so they must be part of the wider group of the disciples. They are not named, but John makes a point of putting them into the account, and why?— because one of them is revealed in verse seven as the young man whom Jesus loved. They then go fishing through the night, and find Jesus on the beach in the morning, and we have the miraculous draught of fishes. Then as in the Passover feast of John 13:22, "one of you shall betray me," in verse 20 John says the same thing, "Peter turning about, sees the disciple whom Jesus loved following, which also leaned on his breast at supper, and said, 'Lord, which is he that betrays you?'" This is in reference to the preceding events at the Passover prior to the crucifixion. We are referring to the same person. This "one following" on the beach does not here appear as a John, as John and James were inseparable and well established in the group of the apostles, and did not need to follow anybody about. The disciple is following Peter and Jesus. It is significant that he is associated with Peter. We all know the feeling of being amongst a new group with only one familiar acquaintance as our friend, the one who invited us, who is talking with the others while we stand close by. This is the sense of the episode on the beach. Here is a man who is an outsider newly come in, as one a little lost in the group, who stays close in company with him who invited him. This can't be John as John knows everyone.

Now here Peter says to Jesus, "Lord, and what shall *this man* do?" Why would he ask such a question if it was regarding John? Those who had been with Jesus from the beginning had a general idea of what the Lord had required of them as the twelve apostles, particularly of James and John, of whom we think of Matthew 19:28 and Mark 10:35-41 where we read:

Jesus said unto them, "Truly I say unto you, That you which have followed me, in the regeneration when the Son of man shall sit in the throne of his glory, you also shall sit upon twelve thrones, judging the twelve tribes of Israel."

And James and John, the sons of Zebedee, came unto him, saying, "Master, we would that you should do for us whatsoever we shall desire." And he said to them, "What would you that I should do for you?" They said to him, "Grant to us that we may sit, one on your right hand, and the other on your left hand, in your glory." But Jesus said to them, "You know not what you ask: can you drink of the cup that I drink of? and be baptized with the baptism that I am baptized with?" And they said unto him, "We can." And Jesus said to them, "You shall indeed drink of the cup that I drink of; and with the baptism that I am baptized withal shall you be baptized: But to sit on my right hand and on my left

| hand is not mine to give; but it shall be given to them for whom it is prepared." And | when the ten heard it, they began to be much displeased with James and John. |

They knew they would all be kings, judges, over God's Israel, but here must be someone who is not of the twelve— "what shall this man do?" Furthermore Mark 3:14 shows us *the twelve* were called to be *preachers*. James and John would drink of the cup that Christ drank of, a privilege of which the others on hearing were much displeased. The apostles' understanding of this cup was coloured by their view of Christ as a king, of which they had ambitions, not as a sufferer, as it actually meant, hence their displeasure at the brothers' seeming good fortune. So it was clear to the disciples, even Peter, that John had a clear calling, of which he needed not ask Christ about. They knew they would rule and bear authority, in fact the others were even displeased about the favour shown James and John. John's future role was clear to all.

Furthermore this "What shall this man do?" seems a superfluous question if it regards John as James and John were regarded *together* as the sons of Zebedee in their discussions—an inseparable pair, but here Peter is asking "and what shall *this man* do?" It was not "what are these *two* to do?" It was a genuine question, Peter had no idea what the man would be doing. Peter and John had been together three years with Christ, and they were partners before that, there was no question in their minds about each other's roles. So the man in question must then be a new disciple, as no discussion has taken place about his role. In Mark we read of "a certain young man" present at the betrayal, as we have adverted to. Here Peter refers to "*this* man." And John refers to the one on Jesus' breast as "the one whom Jesus loved."

Jesus gave James and John the sons of Zebedee, a name, "he surnamed them *Boanerges*, which is 'the sons of thunder,' " their temperament being as would desire to call fire down upon people as in Luke 9:54: "And when his disciples James and John saw this, they said, Lord, will you that we command fire to come down from heaven, and consume them, even as Elijah did?" They were seen as a pair, only to be separated by James' death. They saw themselves in the fashion of prophets like Elijah, ready to call destruction on the enemies of the Lord. They were fishermen, ambitious, loud, brash, rough and temperamental. It seems atypical that such a John be one who rested on the breast of Christ, 14:13-17. As we saw the man on Jesus' bosom at the Passover was referred to by a nick-name, yet John *already* had a nick-name, *Boanerges*, a son of thunder— why should Christ give him another name? Boanerges was a name most suitable to one who would write the Apocalypse, who would call fire and thunder down from heaven, but "the one whom Jesus loved" has no appropriate foundation in John's story and personality.

In preparing the Last Supper Jesus sent two of his disciples—Luke shows they were Peter and John, to make ready for the Passover, telling them to go into the city, to meet a man with a pitcher of water, to follow him into a house with a large upper room furnished and prepared. In the evening it is said he comes with the twelve. It was a *large* upper room, this did not preclude those disciples who were serving the twelve. In John 13

THE ONE WHOM JESUS LOVED

we continue there regarding an imminent betrayal:

"I speak not of you all: I know whom I have chosen: but that the scripture may be fulfilled, He that eats bread with me has lifted up his heel against me. Now I tell you before it come, that, when it is come to pass, you may believe that I am he. Truly, truly, I say to you, He that receives whomsoever I send receives me; and he that receives me receives him that sent me." When Jesus had thus said, he was troubled in spirit, and testified, and said, "Truly, truly, I say unto you, that one of you shall betray me." Then the disciples looked one on another, doubting of whom he spoke. Now there was leaning on Jesus' bosom one of his disciples, whom Jesus loved. Simon Peter therefore beckoned to him, that he should ask who it should be of whom he spoke. He then lying on Jesus' breast said unto him, "Lord, who is it?" Jesus answered, "He it is, to whom I shall give a sop, when I have dipped it." And when he had dipped the sop, he gave it to Judas Iscariot, the son of Simon. And after the sop Satan entered into him. Then said Jesus unto him, "That you do, do quickly." Now no man at the table knew for what intent he spoke this unto him. For some of them thought, because Judas had the bag, that Jesus had said unto him, "Buy those things that we have need of against the feast;" or, that he should give something to the poor. He then having received the sop went immediately out: and it was night.

In Mark 14:18-20, and Matthew 26:20-25 we read how Jesus declares that one of the twelve who were eating with him should betray him. Luke does not observe the chronology with many of the stories compiled in the midst of his gospel, where he changes the order of events here, and places it after the supper: 22:21-23, " 'But, behold, the hand of him that betrays me is with me on the table. And truly the Son of man goes, as it was determined: but woe unto that man by whom he is betrayed!' And they began to enquire among themselves, which of them it was that should do this thing." We can then abide with the other two accounts regarding the chronological order.

All of them begin to ask one by one, "Is it I?" Jesus says, "It is one of the twelve that dips with me in the dish." Matthew shows us that Judas answers the last, after his statement of dipping in the dish, to which Christ replies "You have said." In Mark's account however we have a distinction, "they began to be sorrowful, and to say unto him one by one, 'Is it I?' " followed by, "and *another* said, 'Is it I?' "— *see diagram*. This is followed by, "he answered and said unto them, 'It is one of the twelve that dips with me in the dish.'" The Greek "*auto*" or "them" can mean *him* as well as *them*, so we can regard this as being spoken quietly to "the one whom Jesus loved." In saying "It is one of the twelve," Jesus shows us he is speaking to *another*, beside the twelve, the "*another* said" of verse 19. Matthew merely says "he answered and said." Now Matthew does not make the distinction as Mark does that it was not one of the twelve saying "is it I?", but Mark does because he wants it clear that there is an "*another*" there, as he is giving us subtle facts that relate to himself. In Matthew's account Judas' delayed question "Is it I?" came after the "dips with me in the dish," therefore, this "another" of Mark's gospel is not Judas and it is not one of the twelve but Mark himself. It is extraordinary that all of them, in face of this dark prediction respond with a doubt that they are potentially culpable in this matter of betrayal, in the presence of Christ. It seems a nervy response of tender consciences to the holy One. The one that responds last, who does not react quickly in surprise, is in fact

THE ONE WHOM JESUS LOVED

| Mark 14:17 And in the evening he came with the twelve.
18 And as they sat and did eat, Jesus said, "Truly I say unto you, One of you which eats with me shall betray me."
19 And they began to be sorrowful, *and to say unto him one by one, "Is it I?"* | Matthew 26:20 Now when the even was come, he sat down with the twelve.
21 And as they did eat, he said, "Truly I say unto you, that one of you shall betray me."
22 And they were exceeding sorrowful, *and began every one of them to say to him, "Lord, is it I?"* |

and another said, "Is it I?"

| 20 And he answered and said to them, "It is one of the twelve, that dips with me in the dish.
21 The Son of man indeed goes, as it is written of him: but woe to that man by whom the Son of man is betrayed! good were it for that man if he had never been born." | 23 And he answered and said, "He that dips his hand with me in the dish, the same shall betray me.
24 The Son of man goes as it is written of him: but woe unto that man by whom the Son of man is betrayed! it had been good for that man if he had not been born." |

25 Then Judas, which betrayed him, answered and said, "Master, is it I?" He said to him, "You have said."

| 22 And as they did eat, Jesus took bread, and blessed, and brake it, and gave to them, and said, "Take, eat: this is my body." 23 And he took the cup, and when he had given thanks, he gave it to them: and they all drank of it. 24 And he said to them, "This is my blood of the new testament, which is shed for many." | 26 And as they were eating, Jesus took bread, and blessed it, and brake it, and gave it to the disciples, and said, "Take, eat; this is my body." 27 And he took the cup, and gave thanks, and gave it to them, saying, "Drink you all of it; 28 For this is my blood of the new testament, which is shed for many for the remission of sins." |

the guilty one, Judas. So here we have a very subtle cue to the presence of another player in the narrative at the supper, and significantly, it is recorded by Mark.

The twelve disciples had looked at one another doubting of whom he spake, as it was one of the twelve who would betray him. "Leaning on Jesus' bosom was one of his disciples, whom Jesus loved," writes John. Simon Peter beckons this disciple to ask him who it is. If the betrayer came from the twelve, who were looking on one another, it is unlikely Peter would beckon one of the twelve for an insight to be granted by the Lord, as the particular apostle being asked to ask Christ may well, under this air of suspicion, actually be the betrayer—it must be another disciple, not John, distinct from the twelve.

As we saw earlier Mark is the one who in companionship with Peter wrote the gospel. If the young man is Mark, then I would go further and suggest that he is also the one whom Jesus loved, who leaned on the bosom of Jesus at the last supper, who asked at the beckoning of Peter, "Lord, which is he that betrays you?" In the calling of the rich young ruler we already have the words, "Then Jesus beholding him loved him," This man then is the disciple whom Jesus loved. It is Mark, the companion of Peter and author of the gospel that bears his name.The young man, then, in a respondent beholding, at the very institution of the Eucharist, is beholding the glory of the Lord, while leaning into his bosom. As Christ had said, those who partake of his flesh and blood have eternal life, such was promised to the young man, when he asked "Good Master, what shall I do that I may inherit eternal life?"

THE ONE WHOM JESUS LOVED

And as Jesus said in John 6:

> Whoso eats my flesh, and drinks my blood, has eternal life; and I will raise him up at the last day. For my flesh is meat indeed, and my blood is drink indeed. He that eats my flesh, and drinks my blood, dwells in me, and I in him. As the living Father has sent me, and I live by the Father: so he that eats me, even he shall live by me. This is that bread which came down from heaven: not as your fathers did eat manna, and are dead: he that eats of this bread *shall live for ever.*

Here the one who sought eternal life partakes of it in the supper. "He that eats of this bread shall live forever." This subject of eternal life will come in later.

We can demonstrate this further. We read the account of the third appearance of Jesus after his resurrection, a similar event as occurred in the first calling of Peter, James and John in Luke chapter five, withthe occurrence of a large catch of fish, now again in John 21:

> But when the morning was now come, Jesus stood on the shore: but the disciples knew not that it was Jesus. Then Jesus said to them, "Children, have you any meat?" They answered him, "No." And he said unto them, "Cast the net on the right side of the ship, and you shall find." They cast therefore, and now they were not able to draw it for the multitude of fishes. Therefore that disciple whom Jesus loved said to Peter, "It is the Lord." Now when Simon Peter heard that it was the Lord, he girt his fisher's coat unto him, (for he was naked,) and did cast himself into the sea. And the other disciples came in a little ship; (for they were not far from land, but as it were two hundred cubits,) dragging the net with fishes.

Here the "disciple whom Jesus loved" is in the boat with the others fishing, and he says to Peter, "it is the

Lord." He addresses Jesus as *the Lord*. Here again is another confession of faith in Christ. In the first account they forsook all and followed Christ. Now, it is said that Peter is naked and girts, or gathers his coat about him and jumps into the sea. Why this mention of Peter being naked? Is it a relational allusion, an inside pun, a hint as to the nakedness of the young disciple, that Peter and he have a common interest and calling, as when the blind man casts aside his garment in Mark 10:46-52? In an allegorical sense we observe Peter the fisher of men casting himself into the sea of peoples, clothed with a fisher's coat to catch men, in Luke 5:4-11 we read of the earlier calling of the apostles beside the sea, where in similar fashion after Jesus had told them to launch out into the deep they had inclosed a great multitude of fish. Along with James and John, Peter was astonished at the catch, Simon Peter confessed his sinfulness, but Jesus said to Simon "Fear not, from henceforth you shall catch men." As the young man had been stripped of all his possessions, so Peter has been stripped of all his boasting, awaiting his restoration on the seashore, where after this second draught of fishes, first we read of Christ's discussion with Peter about his love for him, and his call to feed the lambs and sheep, and following this we have the account of "the disciple whom Jesus loved:" again in John 21:

> Then Peter, turning about, sees the disciple whom Jesus loved following; which also leaned on his breast at supper, and said, "Lord, which is he that betrays you?" Peter seeing him said to Jesus, "Lord, and what shall this man do?" Jesus said to him, "If I will that he tarry till I come, what is that to you? you follow me." Then went this saying abroad among the brothers, that that disciple should not die: yet Jesus said

THE ONE WHOM JESUS LOVED

not unto him, "He shall not die;" but, "If I will that he tarry till I come, what is that to you?" [24.] This is the disciple which testifies of these things, and wrote these things: and we know that his testimony is true. And there are also many other things which Jesus did, the which, if they should be written every one, I suppose that even the world itself could not contain the books that should be written. Amen.

In verse 24, John writes, "This is the disciple which testified of these things, and wrote these things: and we know that his testimony is true." The universal view is that John is in reference to himself, as the disciple who leaned on Jesus' bosom, of whom Jesus loved, who wrote *John's* gospel. It is hard to imagine the hardy ambitious John as one who rested on Jesus' bosom. Why would he rest on his bosom? Yet according to the gospel account, a naked young man, later seen in Gethsemene clad in a linen cloth had at some point joined the company of Christ. What would Christ do if such a one came into their midst on a cold night, but offer him the warmth of his robe? So this could only relate to a young man, a youth, perhaps one who has gone through a great difficulty, a great trial, and needs consolation, such would befit a shivering one who rests on His bosom. One who has in following Christ only recently had to leave family, friends and give away his wealth, even most of his clothing, would certainly fit—one such as a shivering young ruler, clad merely in a linen cloth, come out of the cold Passover night.

However, as we have observed, John is a tough competitive fisherman hardened by the sea, a companion of Peter and a brother of James, of whom he is always connected with as the sons of Zebedee, they aspire to be as Elijahs, Jesus calls them *Boanerges*, "the sons of thunder," they are an inseparable pair, with ambitions, and an ambitious mother. Luke 9 says of them,

And they did not receive him, because his face was as though he would go to Jerusalem. And when his disciples James and John saw this, they said, "Lord, do you want us to command fire to come down from heaven, and consume them, even as Elijah did?" But he turned, and rebuked them, and said, "You know not what manner of spirit you are of. For the Son of man is not come to destroy men's lives, but to save them."

Here John and James call for fire from heaven, as Elijah did, on those who did not receive Christ. This would explain, that even in the face of Christ's declaring his death they ask for position at his right hand, as Elijah himself was taken by a fiery chariot to heaven. They had already heard thunder from heaven, and witnessed the miracles of Christ, to expect similar deliverances. It is not without reason that the hostile onlookers at the cross mocked the disciples and Christ regarding an imminent rescue by Elijah, Matthew 27:47-48, who would spare them all, so the disciples must have held that notion. They have a rough harsh spirit, it is hard to imagine such a John with such a manner of spirit as leaning on Jesus' bosom before the events of Jesus' betrayal and sudden death, and that just after the triumphal entry into Jerusalem, when the expectation of the disciples was at a fever pitch.

Peter was asked by Jesus, "Do you love me?" He finds it hard to answer, but hedges, and says in the manner of a hard man who has difficulty saying such things, as if a tough adolescent, "aaw, (averted gaze) you know that I love you," so it is with James and

THE ONE WHOM JESUS LOVED

John, who are cut from the same cloth. The surname of "Sons of Thunder" does not befit a tender bruised youth needing comfort, as the disciple whom Jesus loved rested on his bosom. Such a John would not hesitate to avenge a betrayal.

Furthermore how can John bear witness to himself that *his* own testimony is true, given Jesus' words in John 5:31-32, "If I bear witness of *myself*, my witness is not true." Also John 7:18, "He that speaks of himself seeks his own glory." Who is the "we," of the "*we* know that *his* testimony is true," but John and the other apostles? John is of the "we" referring to the "his." If the master cannot, then John certainly cannot, bear witness to himself. They are bearing witness to *another*. This *other* is the one whom Jesus loved, so this one cannot be John.

6. Another Shall Gird You

~

> "Verily, verily, I say unto you, When you were young, you girded yourself, and walked wherever you would: but when you shall be old, you shall stretch forth your hands, and another shall gird you, and carry you whither you would not." This spake he, signifying by what death he should glorify God. And when he had spoken this, he said unto him, "Follow me."
> —*John 21:18-19*

IT IS TYPICAL of Mark that he wrote of Peter's later response to Jesus, as they left the house toward the Mount of Olives, in Mark 14:29-31, "But Peter said unto him, Although all shall be offended, yet will not I. And Jesus said unto him, 'Truly I say unto you, That this day, even in this night, before the cock crow twice, you shall deny me thrice.' But he spoke the more vehemently, 'If I should die with you, I will not deny you in any wise.' Likewise also said they all."

Godet observes that "in Mark, Peter omits all circumstances which spoke in his favour and brings out only those which showed his humiliation. Mark shows the 'Get you behind me Satan,' but excludes what Matthew speaks to his dignity, 'Thou art Peter and upon this rock I will build my church.' Mark omits the glorious walk of Peter on the water, and he alone records the two warnings given to him by the two cock-crowings, which made the fall of the disciple the more inexcusable. He removes what in Matthew sat with the hundredfold reward of those who left house and lands to follow Christ, that is, the twelve sitting on

ANOTHER SHALL GIRD YOU

thrones judging the twelve tribes of Israel," in Matthew 19:28. And typically Mark *also* removes the "certain ruler" found in Luke, referring to him simply as "one running."

The apostles all had recovered their sense of self-possession after the announcement of the coming betrayal, particularly Peter who had boasted of his steadfastness. Later after the death and resurrection in John 21:15-19, Christ, on the beach, would reassure Peter of his calling despite the weakness displayed in his denying of Christ, with his "Do you love Me?" questions and the command to feed the sheep. Jesus in John 21:7 puts "the one whom he loved" in a close connection with Peter already together on the boat as friends when Jesus called them from the shore. "It is the Lord," says the disciple, and naked Peter gathers his fishers' cloak and leaps into the sea. Jesus asks "Do you love Me?" here in the presence of "the one whom Jesus loved," a now eminent one who had proven his love to Christ by his staying with him through to the arrest, and beyond, as we shall soon observe. It is as if "I love him, he has displayed he loved me—I love you, do you love me?" In response to Jesus' questions, Peter replies, "And he said to him, 'Lord, you know all things; you know that I love you.' Jesus said to him, 'Feed my sheep.'"

In denying Christ, Peter had not taken up the cross with him to the death. Yet this young man had gone through to the point of almost being arrested, fleeing naked, the one whom Jesus loved had responded in a sacrificial love to Christ, going further than Peter in his following Christ; at the Passover he was barely dressed, but at the betrayal he lost all his clothing, having been assaulted by the young men. Here we have this allusion to the nakedness of Peter which allows a subtle comparison to the nakedness of the young man, who had left his linen cloth behind. And here we have these questions regarding the love of Peter to Christ. Jesus tells him to "feed my lambs" and twice says "feed my sheep." One of the lambs he is to feed is standing next to him, that is, Mark. It is to him that he would feed the events, happenings and teachings of the last three years to include in his gospel. From this point John's narrative continues thus in John 21:18-19:

"Truly, truly, I say unto you, When you were young, you girded yourself, and walked wherever you would: but when you shall be old, you shall stretch forth your hands, and another shall gird you, and carry you where you would not." This he spoke, signifying by what death he should glorify God. And when he had spoken this, he said to him, "Follow me."

Peter had just girt himself with a fisher's cloak, as he was naked, and plunged into the sea. As a young man Peter had girded himself and walked where he wished, he had a business which he had run as he wanted, but now life is out of the confines of his will. Perhaps it was Peter who had girded the naked man with clothing, but now Christ tells him another shall gird *him*, and carry him where he would not have wanted to go. He had clothed himself with fishing, it was his life, now he has thrown off his fisher's cloak.

That day on the beach had started with Simon Peter, Thomas called Didymus, and Nathanael of Cana in Galilee, and the sons of Zebedee, and two other of his disciples. "Simon Peter said to them, I go a fishing.

ANOTHER SHALL GIRD YOU

They say unto him, 'We also go with you.' They went forth, and entered into a ship immediately; and that night they caught nothing." Here in this time they are idle and they do what they always have, fishing. But Jesus had said at their calling—"from henceforth you shall catch men." Here is a renewal of this calling, not to fish, but now to feed the sheep, as a shepherd.

In his last letter, 2 Peter 1:4, he is aware of his imminent death, accepting of it, saying, "Knowing that shortly I must put off this my tabernacle, even as our Lord Jesus Christ has showed me." As John had said, "This he spoke, signifying by what death he should glorify God." This is where Christ had shown him, but now "another shall gird you and carry you whither you would not." That he must be the one to put it off implies that he must face a martyrdom, as Christ had endured. He had walked where he would. But this walking where he wished had been curtailed by another element, his fear of death, some things he was not able to do as he had intended. He had told Christ, "Although all shall be offended, yet will not I," and had vehemently said, "If I should die with you, I will not deny you in any wise," yet he had denied him three times. The denying himself to an imminent death had proved that what he would have happened was rather to a self-preservation. But Christ had assured him he would be girded by another and carried where he would not. In his last letter he is assured of his resolve to suffer the putting off his tabernacle. He is ready to face martyrdom. Jesus himself, through his Spirit, would be with him in the trials ahead—"I am with you alway."

Perhaps Peter's "stretching forth of the hands," and

the "carry you where you would not," with the "putting off this my tabernacle," can be explained by a parallel in Jeremiah 10:17-23, where the prophet on hearing the word of the Lord, that he would sling out the inhabitants of the land and distress them, exclaimed his wound, his hurt, his grief to be borne, saying, "*My tabernacle is spoiled,* all my cords are broken, my children are gone forth of me and are not, and there is none *to stretch forth my tent* anymore, and to set up my curtains." Then he says in verse 23, "O LORD, *I know that the way of man is not in himself: it is not in man that walks to direct his steps.*" "You shall stretch forth your hands," meets with "to stretch forth my tent," and "another shall gird you and carry you where you would not," with "it is not in man to direct his steps." Jeremiah was carried in exile to Egypt to die, and Peter to his Babylon, Rome.

God has his means also and here we have an "another," who "shall gird him, and carry him whither he would not," perhaps in an allusion to "*another* disciple" in Mark. When he was young Peter girded himself and walked where he would. "Where he would" was not to the death however, even though he had boasted of it, but to a self preservation in his denial. But his future colleague had already walked where he would not, even as the last shall be first and the first shall be last. Mark's example would prove a spur to Peter. The "carry you whither you would not" regards his denial, figured in the phrase "you would not." He would be strengthened by this "another" to go "where he would not." Perhaps this "another" is Mark's example in mirroring Christ's actions in the cross. In 1 Peter 3:3 Peter eschews rich clothing, such the young man had given away, "Whose adorning let it not be that outward adorning of plaiting the hair, and of wearing of gold, or of putting on of apparel." Mark is the instrument through which Christ would *gird* Peter, that is to gird on garments, as if the one who had given away all his clothing now girds, in metaphorical fashion, Peter's clothing for him. He will *carry* him, help him bear with patience the trials ahead. He was one who had overcome the lure of the filthy lucre, a guard, an example for Peter. In running a race a warrior would gird his loins, a knight would have his page to assist him into his armour, in preparation for battle. Mark, writing the gospel, shows this girding and carrying, where they share the labour and the honour of presenting the gospel to the world. Mark, as Peter's amanuensis or secretary, has carried Peter in the pages of his gospel to the whole world for two millennia to where he would not and could not.

In Luke 9:48-9, John forbade an outsider exorcising with Jesus' name, but Jesus corrects this exclusivity, saying not to forbid such, "He who is not against us is with us." Jesus had only just responded to his disciples' dispute as to who would be the greatest by taking a little child, saying, "Whoever receives this little child in my name receives me, and whoever receives me receives him who sent me. For he who is least among you all will be great." We see this with Peter, after his humiliation following the betrayal, he takes the young Mark on as a father to a son, and in this he receives him who sent the Son of God, that is, the Father. In this Peter becomes great, it is not without reason that he was given the keys of the kingdom, and plays a seminal role as a pillar in the formation of the church.

7. The Disciple Which Testified

Then Peter, turning about, saw the disciple whom Jesus loved following; which also leaned on his breast at supper, and said, "Lord, which is he that betrays you?" Peter seeing him said to Jesus, "Lord, and what shall this man do?" Jesus said to him, "If I will that he tarry till I come, what is that to you? you follow me." Then went this saying abroad among the brothers, that that disciple should not die: yet Jesus said not to him, "He shall not die;" but, "If I will that he tarry till I come, what is that to you?" This is the disciple which testified of these things, and wrote these things: and we know that his testimony is true.
—*John 21:20-24*

S*T. JOHN SPEAKS* of "the disciple which testified of these things and wrote these things." Commonly this is identified as John. But such a one could only be *Mark*, the companion of Peter, the testifier and writer of the *gospel story*. It cannot be Matthew, for John does not say *"the apostle,"* as John or Matthew is, but "the *disciple*," as Mark is. Here John is adverting to another, that is, the writer of the gospel of *Mark*. John wrote his gospel much time after Mark and Luke, after the fall of Jerusalem. Here John is writing in reference to something already well known, who had already "wrote these things," that is, Mark's gospel, whereas John's gospel is still flowing wet from his quill, none had read it as yet, as the last verse with its *"Amen"* was yet to be written, it can have had no readership, no *"we"* has yet testified to its veracity. The subject here

THE DISCIPLE WHICH TESTIFIED

is the disciple which *testified*, which *wrote*, past tense, one with a reputation of having previously written *these things*, unlike John's gospel, *things* then commonly known and already public. Peter had testified to the writings of Paul, in 2 Peter 3:15, "And account that the longsuffering of our Lord is salvation; even as our beloved brother Paul also according to the wisdom given to him has written to you." So in like manner the apostle John testifies to the evangelist Mark.

Professor Godet[1] writes regarding the formation, and date, of Mark's gospel: "Clement, the future Bishop of Rome, says that while Peter was preaching in Rome, his listeners asked Mark who had for some time accompanied him, and who remembered all that Peter had said, to write down the things related by him, and when written to send it to those who asked for it, so in Rome about 64 AD Mark drew up his work, shortly before the persecution of Nero to which Peter fell a victim in August of that year. While Matthew's gospel was addressed to the Jews, with many prophecy quotations, Mark's gospel is for the Gentiles, and unlike Matthew he explains Jewish customs, and uses words of Latin origin. In the Passion account in Matthew 27:32, and Mark 15:21, Simon of Cyrene is described as the father of Alexander and Rufus. The two sons of Simon lived in Rome, as Paul writes, in Romans 16:13, "Rufus, chosen in the Lord, and his mother and mine." Paul, who had known them in the east, sends his greeting to them in that city. The sons of Simon, of whom one at least held an influential position

---

1. *Studies On The New Testament,* Prof. F. Godet, D.D. Hodder and Stoughton, 1873

in the church of Rome, were still living; Mark honoured them by writing of Simon in the gospel. The date the gospel was composed is established by these facts. The apostolic age was, therefore, not very far advanced. Since the warning of the destruction of Jerusalem, as occurred in the year 70, is found in Mark 13:14, as well as in Matthew, the beginning of the war, 66, had not yet struck. Thus it would be about the year 64, or 65 that the gospel must be dated."

We have demonstrated that this disciple which testified of these things in John's reference is Mark. Here John tells us he is a witness—he has "testified," which *Thayer's Lexicon* tells us is "to affirm that one has seen or heard or experienced something, or that he knows it because taught by divine revelation or inspiration." The surname "Mark" means "defence" in Latin, "to vindicate, to speak or write in favour of." Mark is Peter's companion and *amanuensis*—his writer, his secretary, he wrote the gospel as he has heard it from Peter. Yet not only this, he is also a *particular* witness to Christ, in which he has contributed to his gospel as a primary witness, indeed a most significant witness, as we can demonstrate.

First, as we have already established, he has encountered Christ, and Christ had called him to follow him, as he was "the rich young man." In this he is a witness. And second, John writes that "Peter turns about, sees the disciple whom Jesus loved following, which also leaned on his breast at supper, and said, 'Lord which is he that betrays you?'" So he is identified as the one who testified as to *the identity of the betrayer*—Judas. "This is the disciple which testified of *these* things," writes John. What *things*? *Things* he has just referred to a few verses previously, as he who leaned on the bosom of Jesus at the last supper, who had asked, *"Lord which is he that betrays you?"* John makes a point of defining this one as asking *this* question, not merely as the one who leaned on his bosom, but also who asked *the question* inquiring the identity of the betrayer. Jesus then said, "He it is, to whom I shall give a sop, when I have dipped it. And when he had dipped the sop, he gave it to Judas Iscariot, the son of Simon." This was something that only *Mark* knew. Peter had beckoned to *him* to ask Christ, but Mark did not tell Peter. Peter and the others had no idea Judas was the traitor, as they thought Judas was shopping, as John 13:28-29 recounts:

> Now no man *at the table* knew for what intent he spoke this unto him. For some of them thought, because Judas had the bag, that Jesus had said unto him, "Buy those things that we have need of against the feast;" or, that he should give something to the poor.

One did know, the one who heard, "he it is to whom I give the sop" but here "no man at the table," that is, *none of the official party*, the eleven, knew. It was not until the betrayal in Gethsemane that the others knew. So in chapter 14:43 we read:

> And immediately, while he yet spoke, comes Judas, one of the twelve, and with him a great multitude with swords and staves, from the chief priests and the scribes and the elders,

The phrase "comes Judas" shows a more knowing expectant coming for Mark, who alone was privy to the identity of the betrayer, in seeing Judas entering into

THERE CAME ONE RUNNING

Gethsemane he knew what was about to happen *before* the others. He knew that it was *Judas* who would come. He mentions Judas before he mentions the multitude as he knows who is leading it—he is the one who knows the identity of the betrayer.

If the one whom Jesus loved was John then the close relation he bore to James and Peter, together with his fiery nature, as one who would call fire from heaven, would have seen him share the identity of the traitor with the other disciples immediately, in order to arrest Judas in his intent, before he could leave, if not violently avenge himself upon him. But if the one whom Jesus loved was Mark, the young ruler, then his secret would not have been so easily exposed to the others of whom Mark had formed no close relation as yet, ones who would yet hold some suspicion of a newcomer. This element of suspicion is something of which Christ warned them in his parable of the labourers. The intent in which Christ told this man the identity of the betrayer conveyed to him that he had not to reveal it to others, even to Peter who had asked him to ask the question.

Here the first shall be last and the last first, that is in this instance, the first and the last to know the answer to this question—Who would betray Christ to the death? What was hidden to Peter and the rest is made known to the young man. It is plain that Peter was not told by the young man as Peter also would have fought against Judas, clearly he would not hesitate to use a sword against him, as he would indeed cut off Malchus' ear later in Gethsemane. After all, "*it was written*" in the prophets, so Judas *had* to get away with it. Jesus, as a lamb to the slaughter, would not let them know.

THE DISCIPLE WHICH TESTIFIED

Psalm 41:9 reads "Yea, mine own familiar friend, in whom I trusted, which did eat of my bread, has lifted up his heel against me," and this is recited by Jesus in John 13:18, "I speak not of you all: I know whom I have chosen: but that the scripture may be fulfilled, 'He that eats bread with me has lifted up his heel against me.'" The scripture must be fulfilled. It had to be a familiar friend in whom he had trusted, one of the twelve, not a new convert. With Judas we have a disciple that came first, but now he is the very last, as he has sought to betray his master. Mark was last and has come first, as he rests on the bosom of Jesus, and is privy to the confidence of Christ regarding the identity of the traitor, unlike any of the eleven remaining apostles. The wealthy one who has given away *all* that he has to attain eternal life, is told of the identity of the traitor, while the lover of the purse, he who holds the bag, who has gained thirty pieces of silver for his reward, sets out to buy and acquire *things,* but would lose every thing. The one who had given away everything he had to the poor is contrasted with the one who went away shopping. Here is a great irony. Mark possessed unique treasures of knowledge.

This disciple is stated here to be the one which *both* "testified of these things *and* wrote these things." Here John is speaking of one who was generally known by John's readers, as having written and testified of certain things, that is, as we have seen, regarding the identity of the betrayer. This could only have been Mark, as his gospel was then current and well known at the time John wrote his gospel. Perhaps it is that that disciple, that is Mark, had indeed fallen asleep, before the writing of John's gospel, or died, as Peter had done at Rome, perhaps with him, and that this word of John would confirm that the saying among the brothers, of that disciple's immortality was *not* what Jesus had meant, but nevertheless his gospel is true. Here we have come to the conclusion that Mark is the one being the object of John's reference, and not John himself. John says "we know that his testimony is true," a testimony attested by his having written. John cannot be making reference to himself as he has not set the seal to the publishing and launching of his gospel as he is in fact still in the act of writing it. John is referring to another already current and known at the time of his writing his gospel. Another perhaps who has fallen asleep in martyrdom, with his father Peter, of whom whose story can now be hinted at.

John refers to "the disciple which testified," that is, Mark with his gospel, and he intimates that there are many other things Jesus did, and that these books should be written. *John's* gospel then is an answer to this desire, a book that should be written. Yet we also have an oblique reference to this hidden history of this disciple, a book that should be written, a story untold yet told already between the lines, even as this book reveals. These other things Jesus did are unfolded to us in the hints that John provides in his gospel. It is John who finally after the death of the others, provides a key for us to open these stories in the other gospels.

8. If I Will That He Tarry

Then Peter, turning about, sees the disciple whom Jesus loved following; which also leaned on his breast at supper, and said, "Lord, which is he that betrays you?" Peter seeing him said to Jesus, "Lord, and what shall this man do?" Jesus said unto him, "If I will that he tarry till I come, what is that to you? you follow me." Then went this saying abroad among the brothers, that that disciple should not die: yet Jesus said not unto him, "He shall not die;" but, "If I will that he tarry till I come, what is that to you?" This is the disciple which testifies of these things, and wrote these things: and we know that his testimony is true. And there are also many other things which Jesus did, the which, if they should be written every one, I suppose that even the world itself could not contain the books that should be written. Amen.
—*John 21:20-25*

WE HAVE CONSIDERED who is the disciple which testified of these things, now we shall look at another element in this same passage, "If I will that he tarry till I come what is that to you?"

Let us now consider the beach episode in John 21 further, as it adds to the story. Now here in verse 22, on the beach, Jesus responds to Peter's question regarding the one whom Jesus loved, "What shall this man do?" with, "If I will that he tarry till I come, what is that to you? You follow me." This word is a riddle for them to chew over, particularly for Peter, as it regards his future companion, even his "*son*."

The answer for Peter would be found in the parable

of the labourers of which Jesus is referring to, as implied in the words "tarry," and "standing idle," which was told to them earlier, immediately after the invitation to the young man, and the discussion on the rich man getting into the kingdom. We have the word in the parable, referring to the later admission of workers into the vineyard in Matthew 20:

> And about the eleventh hour he went out, and found others standing idle, and said to them, Why do you stand here all the day idle? They say to him, Because no man has hired us. He says to them, You go also into the vineyard; and whatsoever is right, that shall you receive.

Now commonly the *he* of Peter's interrogatory of Christ on the beach is taken today as referring to John, as some have it, that is that John would abide, or "tarry till I come," that is, abide in the world till the revealing of the Apocalypse, that he would not die till Christ's coming to John in that Revelation. Tales of John having survived boiling in oil in a kind of martyrdom are attempts to elaborate on this view. But this man, as we have demonstrated, is that disciple that testifies of the betrayal, which is Mark, the disciple whom Jesus loved. The "brothers," of whom the saying "that he would not die" became current, themselves knew of whom they were speaking, which as we have shown is actually Mark, the rich young man, and not John. But they were under a mistaken apprehension of Christ's words to Peter of the phrase "if I will that he tarry till I come," as referring to Christ's future coming, when Christ was actually referring to the past, to the calling of this eminent disciple, as Christ *came* to him, as the owner employing him into the vineyard—which had

IF I WILL THAT HE TARRY

already happened with the following of the disciple into the first Eucharist, in the large upper room. The young man had come to Christ desiring eternal life. Unlike other inquirers he is not received immediately into their midst in a "follow thou me;" rather in this case he is given conditions. He is to give away his wealth. He is told "go your way," *hupago*, that is withdraw oneself. He is not to join the disciples as yet. He is a labourer standing idle, but in his case the householder of the vineyard has not called him into the labouring, at least until he has sold what he has and given to the poor. He is to continue to stand idle in terms of employment in the vineyard, or in other words, he is to "tarry till I come." In a sense the disciple came into the vineyard at the Passover, the very first Eucharist, where he would drink of the very wine of the vineyard, as it was recorded of the one whom Jesus loved. *Mark*, in 14:17 says regarding the Passover meeting, "And in the evening he *comes* with the twelve." Here it is said of Christ that he *comes*. And it is here that the labourer tarries *till he comes*, that is joins in with his band as a follower. As we saw earlier, it was Peter and John who had prepared the large upper room for the feast. John was not in need of the warmth of Christ's robe that night, as he was one prepared for it. Mark however was cold, having given away all he had, wearing only a thin linen garment. When Christ comes to him he embraces him, indeed gives him the shared warmth of his robe on a dark cold night.

These words of the disciple that should not die were a riddle for *Peter*, of which *he* was to seek meaning, as the young man would have a *particular* significance

THERE CAME ONE RUNNING

in Peter's life. The saying was hidden to others, to the brothers, whom Christ would suffer their own false conclusions as to the meaning. After all, "what is that to you" applies more equally to them than even Peter. At the first the young man had questioned Christ how to attain *eternal life*, and Christ had answered, "Give away all you have and follow me, etc.," this he had done, in spite of all those who had doubted such a one to follow Christ, and in this connection it is natural to assume some to conclude that he would not die, as he had indeed done as Christ had said—given away all he had, and therefore would logically possess the eternal life and not suffer death, as Christ had expressly promised when he called him. The calling of Mark would seem a remarkable thing in the circle of the apostles, with his "impossible" calling, his insight into Judas' betrayal of Christ at the Passover, his presence at the betrayal, and even more things which we shall examine later, and so it would be natural that much discussion and supposition among the disciples would take place regarding the words of Christ in this respect as it bore on this extraordinary conversion, to wit the "immortality" of Mark, and the credulity of the disciples, all this given the extraordinary times they lived in, the expectancy of the Messiah and his kingdom, with its New Covenant, the imminent end of the world, the presence of Christ among them with his personality, wisdom and miracles, the raising of Lazarus, all of this would contribute to their also holding to some other extraordinary and even fantastical notions.

Now the phrase, "If I will that he tarry," has respect to those in the parable "standing idle" outside the

IF I WILL THAT HE TARRY

vineyard. To this class is the rich young man, Simon of Cyrene, who carried the cross, and the repentant thief, just before his death. Here they come into the story, *late*, until *Christ come* and call them. He is not hired by the householder immediately, he tarries. *He is to tarry till Christ comes.* He is all one with the others standing idle, whom no man had hired. Jesus had said of him, of whom no *man* had hired, "With men it is impossible, but not with God: for *with God* all things are possible."

In addition he says "that *disciple* should not die." There are *disciples* mentioned in the gospel, that is, those two on the beach, and these as distinct from the apostles who are mentioned by name. It is referring to a particular *disciple*, not an *apostle*, or a John. However, at any rate, the idea that John or any other disciple would not die is expressly denied by John as being the case in point, as here: "yet Jesus *said not* to him, He shall not die; but, If I will that he tarry till I come, what is that to you?" Christ is actually saying that it is not that Mark should not die but simply and solely, "If I will that he tarry till I come, what is that to you?" John is saying Jesus is referring only to this statement, not the notion they had held of an immortal disciple.

Now Jesus answers Peter's "What shall this man do?" with the question, "If I will that he tarry till I come what is that to you?" Compare this with the parable:

So when evening was come, the lord of the vineyard said unto his steward, Call the labourers, and give them their hire, beginning from the last to the first. And when they came that were hired about the eleventh hour, they received every man a penny. But when the first came, they supposed that they should have received more; and they likewise received every man a penny. And when they had

THERE CAME ONE RUNNING

received it, they murmured against the goodman of the house, Saying, These last have wrought but one hour, and you have made them equal to us, which have borne the burden and heat of the day. But he answered one of them, and said, Friend, I do you no wrong: did not you agree with me for a penny? Take that is yours, and go your way: I will give to this last, even as to you. Is it not lawful for me to do what I will with my own? Is your eye evil, because I am good? So the last shall be first, and the first last: for many be called, but few chosen.

Here they suppose they should receive more than those who have wrought but one hour. Christ's "What is that to you?" contrasts with the goodman's, "Is it not lawful for me to do what I want with my own?" The question to the ruler, "Why do you call me good?" agrees with "the goodman of the house."

In another sense we see this disciple tarrying till Christ comes. One can draw a comparison with the payment of the parable with Christ's invitation to the apostolic band to dine with him on the beach:

> Jesus said to them, Come and dine. And none of the disciples dared ask him, Who are you? knowing that it was the Lord. Jesus then comes, and takes bread, and gives them, and fish likewise. This is now the third time that Jesus showed himself to his disciples, after that he was risen from the dead.

The disciples are tarrying on the beach, having nothing to do, they go fishing, then Jesus shows himself to them on the shore, after the catch of fish, and it is said there, "Jesus *then comes*, and takes bread, and gives them, and fish likewise." This disciple thus tarries till he *comes*. Christ comes once more to the disciple. Here on the beach is a glorious climax to the resurrection, the three years of Christ's public showing among the nation,

IF I WILL THAT HE TARRY

his companionship with his followers, and the great relief—the Lord is risen among them, after the great ordeal that he and they had endured. Here is not a casual happening but a significant event. It is a resurrection feast, an intermission in the ages, in anticipation of the future wedding banquet at the end of the age, before the giving of the Holy Spirit at Pentecost. The labourers, the apostolic band are receiving their hire, their *penny*. Here the faithful labourers are receiving a gift of fish from Christ, an equal reward, a great draught of fish, a meal cooked by him on the beach. Coin and fish meet in Matthew 17:27, which reads: "Go to the sea, and cast an hook, and take up the fish that first comes up; and when you have opened his mouth, you shall find a piece of money." And here Jesus gives to this last what he gives to the first.

9. What Shall This Man Do?

Then Peter, turning about, sees the disciple whom Jesus loved following; which also leaned on his breast at supper, and said, "Lord, which is he that betrays you?" Peter seeing him said to Jesus, "Lord, and what shall this man do?" Jesus said to him, "If I will that he tarry till I come, what is that to you? You follow me." Then went this saying abroad among the brothers, that that disciple should not die: yet Jesus said not to him, "He shall not die;" but, "If I will that he tarry till I come, what is that to you?" This is the disciple which testifies of these things, and wrote these things: and we know that his testimony is true. And there are also many other things which Jesus did, the which, if they should be written every one, I suppose that even the world itself could not contain the books that should be written. Amen.
—*John 21:20-25*

Here we shall examine yet another element in this passage regarding Peter's question, "What shall this man do?" The twelve apostles and the disciples had been with Christ for three years. Some had come early, others within that period. Even as the parable said, some came to work in the vineyard early in the morning, or others in the third hour, the sixth, the ninth, and the eleventh. Christ had taught them many things, and they had seen many miracles and debates and conflicts. Peter sees this new disciple at the Passover, on the boat and the beach come among them, one come at the eleventh hour, as one who has wrought but one hour, one who has been standing idle, so to speak, now made equal to the apostles, who have borne the burden and heat of the day. Mark's equality with the others shows itself in that he has been shown the identity of the betrayer, before the knowing of the apostles themselves. Peter had been denied the knowledge of Judas' treachery, yet this man lastly called had been privy to the identity of the traitor. And Mark has shown more courage than the apostles, as he was the last to flee from the multitude at the betrayal, even after the apostles had fled. Here on the beach it appears that Peter, who had denied Christ, has a more than passing curiosity in this lad. He is fascinated despite himself, "What shall this man do?" he needs to know, and Jesus, while knowing the future relation these two would hold, yet discourages Peter's interest on it, saying, "if I will that he tarry till I come, *what is that to you?* You follow me."

In the parable those who came first and worked the whole day, as had Peter, one first to be called, complained, "These last have wrought but one hour, and you have made them equal unto us, which have borne the burden and heat of the day." The answer given them was, "But he answered one of them, and said, Friend, I do you no wrong: did not you agree with me for a penny? Take that is yours and go your way, I will give unto this last, even as unto you."

It is said he answers "one of them," as we see this has an especial concern for Peter, with his questions, who is the one who busybodies himself in regard to the disciple whom Jesus loved who has been made equal to him. Jesus discourages him in this trait, with his response, "What is that to you?" It was Peter who had showed such curiosity regarding the disciple in asking the question at the Passover. As we have seen Mark would be Peter's companion in the preaching of the gospel, he would be the one to write the gospel, under the direction of Peter, and yet also act as a first hand witness in other things, as will become apparent in later chapters. What was given to this one called into the labours last, was that given also unto Peter. In fact the converse is also true, what was given unto this man would also be given to Peter as we will see.

Now Christ says in the parable, "Is it not lawful for me to do what I will with my own? Is your eye evil because I am good?" Here we see the goodness of God to Mark, eyed narrowly by Peter, the blessings on the late are seen as unfair by those called early. The disciples were such as would deny children and blind men access to Jesus, they were ambitious men, they had this elitist competitive spirit, given to jealousy over the domain of others, as the young man had observed in the events regarding the children coming to Christ, and perhaps from afar when the blind beggar was called. Christ, through this parable and the events of the passion, would seek to remove this weakness, so that when it came to the calling and confirmation of Paul, and the incoming of the Gentiles, they were prepared to humbly receive all that Christ had called into his kingdom.

But to this "to do what I will" of the parable agrees the "if I will ~ what is that to you?" on the beach. Notice the word "will":

WHAT SHALL THIS MAN DO?

Christ on the beach
"If I will that he tarry till I come, what is that to you?"

Parable of the labourers
"Is it not lawful for me to do what I will with my own?"

Christ does what he wills with his own. Now notice how the word "good" knits in with the following words to the young ruler.

Parable of the labourers
"Is your eye evil because I am good?"

The calling of the young man
"Why do you call me good? there is none good but God."

As the parable forms a relation to Christ's will on the beach regarding the young man so here the parable forms a relation with the young man's calling. This is then closed with the phrase in verse 16, "So the last shall be first, and the first last: for many be called, but few chosen." So it is the young man called last, who would prove to be first; the rich young ruler, who had gone away sorrowful for he had many possessions, who would prove to be among the chosen. The apostle who holds the bag would be cast out, while the rich ruler would be brought in. Notice that the lord of the vineyard is also called the *goodman* of the house.

The answer to Peter's question then, "What shall this man do?" regarding this disciple, was found in the parable, particularly the words, "I will give unto this last, even as unto you." It is as if Christ is saying "I have called this one a labourer late into the vineyard, who shall receive the same rewards and payment as Peter and the others, receive him therefore as your own." Indeed what is given to all the apostles is displayed and made known in Mark's gospel. Here we are seeing a significant addition to the band of the apostles, the evangelist Mark, in his role as the companion and *amanuensis* of Peter. The gospel of Peter would be the gospel of Mark. It is like an Aaron with Moses. Peter is fascinated with the destiny of this young man, as he would be predestined a close companion to him, what would be given Peter would also be given Mark, as true yoke-fellows. Yet Jesus had also said, "If I will that he tarry till I come what is that to you? You follow me." The first phrase, the "tarrying till I come" gives Peter the clue to the riddle as resting in the words of the parable. The calling late of this disciple has no bearing on the young man's standing with the apostolic band as if it were inferior or of no consequence. Peter's position is to be found in following Christ, but Mark's status is linked into his position as a son to a father in Peter. Mark is to follow the lead of Peter, as Peter follows Christ.

Peter is a self made man, an independent fisherman, a man of great curiosity, self-willed, he finds it hard to follow at times, and Jesus' riddle-word to him on the beach regarding his death speak to this tendency in him, as we read in John 21: "Truly, truly, I say unto you, When you were young, you girded yourself, and walked wherever you would: but when you shall be old, you shall stretch forth your hands, and another shall gird you, and carry you whither you would not." Peter is to follow Christ, and Mark is to follow Peter, so the role of Mark is to Peter a "What is that to you? You follow me."

Peter writes, as one who has learned, in his first letter, "But let none of you suffer as a murderer, or as a thief, or as an evildoer, or as a busybody in other men's matters." With regard to the betrayal, Peter had asked, with the others, "Is it I?" but he was not the murderer, or the thief, he was perhaps an evildoer with his denial, but certainly he was the *busybody*, as shown in his persistent questions.

The parable of the labourers in the vineyard is thus stitched together with the story of this young man and Peter in a curiously prophetic and descriptive fashion.

So Mark becomes a companion of Peter, a writer of the gospel with him. He is one of the lambs that Christ has told Peter to feed with the gospel, verse 15, "Do you love me more than these?" Among the *these* is the Mark upon the beach. Indeed it was to Mark that Peter entrusted the teaching and stories of the past three years in a feeding of the lambs, made manifest in his gospel, much of it was given by Peter to Mark, before it was imparted to us. "He said to him, Yes, Lord; you know that I love you. He said to him, Feed my lambs." Love and loyalty to Christ must come before others if Peter is to be a true shepherd— "You follow me" sets the standard. Peter's concerns must be first for Christ, *then* for the flock. He wrote as one who had denied Christ but found mercy, "For you were as sheep going astray; but are now returned to the Shepherd and Bishop of your souls." The concern for the flock is also tempered with the knowledge that Christ is their shepherd also, "If I will that he tarry, what is that to you, you follow me," and, "Is it not lawful for me *to do what I will* with mine own?" Peter is given the charge to care for the one whom Jesus loved, he is to be a father to him, as another was given the care of his mother Mary. Peter, as proved in the account of his dissembling with Judaizers of which Paul opposed in the Acts, was given to the weakness of being influenced by inferiors, when he should have taken the lead. This "what is that to you," then, serves as a precedent to him to not be concerned with the opinions of followers but to immediately follow Christ himself as his apostle, as befits the one holding the Keys. He would write, "If any man speak, let him speak as the oracles of God." Mark was a ruler, and his actions in following Christ showed an independence to the hesitancy and timidity of the apostles, and a familiarity in taking the lead. Such a man would prove an example to Peter.

Peter also wrote in his epistle, of things which we take notice of, that is, the humility in leadership, the disdain for money, the witness to Christ's sufferings, the assumption of oversight placed upon him, the necessity of a ready mind, all things that pertain to the lessons learned in the time of the Passion:

> The elders which are among you I exhort, who am also an elder, and a witness of the sufferings of Christ, and also a partaker of the glory that shall be revealed: Feed the flock of God which is among you, taking the oversight thereof, not by constraint, but willingly; not for filthy lucre, but of a ready mind; Neither as being lords over God's heritage, but being ensamples to the flock. And when the chief Shepherd shall appear, you shall receive a crown of glory that fades not away.

The company of one who had given away riches, once a *young ruler*, would prove an enduring testimony to Peter to not be tempted by the filthy lucre. This period was a seminal time for the apostles, of which much was burned into their souls, of which they would ever after spend meditating upon. This would result in much care

WHAT SHALL THIS MAN DO?

and subtlety in their recounting the events. John supplies this phrase regarding Mark in verse 24, "This is the disciple which testified of these things, and wrote these things: and we know that his testimony is true." In other words, what does this man do? he writes *the gospel of Mark*. This disciple testifies that "the Son of man indeed goes," 14:21, "as it is written of him," and verse 41, "*the hour is come*; behold, the Son of man is betrayed into the hands of sinners." Mark is the pre-eminent witness to the act that was foretold in the prophets—the betrayal of Christ to his death, and as we will soon see, much more besides. It was John the Baptist who revealed the coming of the Lamb of God, while it was Mark who bore testimony to the betrayal.

10. Testifying to *These* Things

> Then Peter, turning about, sees the disciple whom Jesus loved following; which also leaned on his breast at supper, and said, "Lord, which is he that betrays you?" Peter seeing him said to Jesus, "Lord, and what shall this man do?" Jesus said unto him, "If I will that he tarry till I come, what is that to you? You follow me." Then went this saying abroad among the brothers, that that disciple should not die: yet Jesus said not to him, "He shall not die;" but, "If I will that he tarry till I come, what is that to you?" This is the disciple which testifies of these things, and wrote these things: and we know that his testimony is true.
> *—John 21:20-24*

AS WE HAVE seen Mark is the one who has testified as to *the identity of the betrayer*—Judas. "This is the disciple which testified of *these* things," writes John. Such things were prophesied in the Old Testament, and referred to by Christ himself as being imminent, at the very door. In Mark chapters 8:31, 38, 9:9-12, 31, and in 10:33-34 Christ has intimated his death at the hands of the authorities, and his resurrection.

> Saying, "Behold, we go up to Jerusalem; and the Son of man shall be delivered to the chief priests, and to the scribes; and they shall condemn him to death, and shall deliver him to the Gentiles: And they shall mock him, and shall scourge him, and shall spit upon him, and shall kill him: and the third day he shall rise again."

Luke the physician, in chapter 22:44 records the

scene of the betrayal where Christ, "being in an agony he prayed more earnestly: and his sweat was as it were great drops of blood falling down to the ground." He speaks of an angel strengthening him. And in the account of Mark 14:32-42, immediate to the coming of Judas, we have the story of the sleeping apostles, and the prayers of Christ are recounted. Finally we read, "Sleep on now, and take your rest: it is enough, the hour is come; behold, the Son of man is betrayed into the hands of sinners. Rise up, let us go; lo, he that betrays me is at hand." Mark was expectant of this betrayal, therefore he would not have slept, he is the witness to it, here we must be reading a first hand account of the events in Gethsemane. Mark 14:34 reads, "And (Jesus) said to them, My soul is exceeding sorrowful unto death;" While in Psalm 55:4 we have, "My heart is sore pained within me: and the terrors of death are fallen upon me. Fearfulness and trembling are come upon me, and horror has overwhelmed me." In verse 9 we have "violence and strife in the city," attended with mischief and sorrow, wickedness, deceit and guile in the midst. Then the Psalmist declares in verse 12, "For it was not an enemy that reproached me; then I could have borne it: neither was it he that hated me that did magnify himself against me; then I would have hid myself from him: But it was you, a man mine equal, my guide (intimate friend) and mine acquaintance. We took sweet counsel together, and walked to the house of God in company."

Here in the Psalm we see prophesied the heart of the betrayal, while in Zechariah 11:12 we have some facts and figures, "So they weighed for my price thirty pieces of silver. And the LORD said to me, "Cast it to the potter: a goodly price that I was prised at of them." And I took the thirty pieces of silver, and cast them to the potter in the house of the LORD." In the Septuagint "to the potter" translates as "into the furnace," the kiln. In the Psalm, verse 15, the judgment falls quickly on the wicked, as it in fact did fall upon Judas in the potter's field, the furnace, "Let death seize upon them, and let them go down quick into hell: for wickedness is in their dwellings, and among them."

This all relates to the *proto-evangelion* of Genesis 3:15, the mother of all prophecies, where God promised a saviour in response to the fall in Eden:

> And I will put enmity between you and the woman, and between your seed and her seed; it shall bruise your head, and you shall bruise his heel.

This testifying of the betrayer is the bearing witness to the initiation of that great and ancient promise. Man had given away his glory, to stand naked, as Adam said, "I was naked; and I hid myself," and now one who had given away all he had, a naked man who had fled, was given sole insight in a witness to the beginning of this event, where the glory would be restored to fallen humanity. As Mary Magdalene had anointed Christ to the burial in the house of Bethany, this young new disciple serves as a confidante in the horror that Christ now faces. Such a secret shared was a support to Jesus, in the loneliness of his task. Christ had said he was "straitened to accomplish his baptism," as if he were a sacrificial animal hemmed in to certain death, the young man thus takes up the cross with him as one who

TESTIFYING TO THESE THINGS

knows something more of the betrayal than the others.

This knowledge then, given to the one whom Jesus loved, was no mere minor tidbit. It was the hinge on which mighty doors did turn. It was the fulfilment of the ancient prophecies. Peter wrote, in his first letter chapter 1:10-12,

> Of which salvation the prophets have enquired and searched diligently, who prophesied of the grace that should come to you: Searching what, or what manner of time the Spirit of Christ which was in them did signify, when it testified beforehand the sufferings of Christ, and the glory that should follow. Unto whom it was revealed, that not unto themselves, but *unto us* they did minister the things, which are now reported unto you by them that have preached the gospel unto you with the Holy Ghost sent down from heaven; which things the angels desire to look into.

Here Peter and his companions have stated an astonishing thing, they *themselves* are the witnesses and recipients of the salvation the ancient prophets testified, "*unto us*." He is not talking of his readers, when he says "unto us," as he qualifies in the ensuing sentence, "which are *now reported* unto *you*," but is referring to the actual witnesses of the events, the disciples. And of course this "us" includes in an eminent fashion, the evangelist Mark. He also wrote, in verses 16-21,

> For we have not followed cunningly devised fables, when we made known unto you the power and coming of our Lord Jesus Christ, but were eyewitnesses of his majesty. For he received from God the Father honour and glory, when there came such a voice to him from the excellent glory, "This is my beloved Son, in whom I am well pleased." And this voice which came from heaven we heard, when we were with him in the holy mount.

This also refers to the transfiguration which he, James and John were privileged to have seen, where Moses and Elijah appeared and Christ "transfigured before them and his raiment became shining, exceeding white as snow; so as no fuller on earth can white them," "and a voice came out of the cloud, saying, This is my beloved Son: hear him," as Peter records through Mark. Then in his letter he says, "We have also a more sure word of prophecy; whereunto you do well that you take heed, as to a light that shines in a dark place, until the day dawn, and the day star arise in your hearts: Knowing this first, that no prophecy of the scripture is of any private interpretation. For the prophecy came not in old time by the will of man: but holy men of God spoke as they were moved by the Holy Ghost." And so the apostles and disciples were witnesses to the fulfilment of many prophecies.

Compare Psalm 69:21, 30: "They gave me also gall for my meat; and in my thirst they gave me vinegar to drink. . . I will praise the name of God with a song, and will magnify him with thanksgiving," with the supper in Mark 14:25-26, "I will drink no more of the fruit of the vine, until that day that I drink it new in the kingdom of God. And when they had sung an hymn, they went out into the mount of Olives." John tells us the time when this was accomplished, "Now there was set a vessel full of vinegar: and they filled a sponge with vinegar, and put it upon hyssop, and put it to his mouth. When Jesus therefore had received the vinegar, (sour wine and water) he said, It is finished: and he bowed his head, and gave up the ghost." Here as Luke 19:12 says, when we have "A certain nobleman went into a far country to receive for himself a kingdom, and to return." Jesus had said to Pilate, "My kingdom is not of this world," and Peter declares to all in Acts 2:32-33, 35, "This Jesus has God raised up, whereof we all are witnesses. Therefore being by the right hand of God exalted . . . God has made that same Jesus, whom you have crucified, both Lord and Christ."

When the Greeks came to worship at the feast in John 13:20, they came to Philip with their desire to see Jesus, which Jesus refused. The wall of partition still separated the Gentiles from Christ and his Israel. Although certain exceptions pre-typified the incoming of the Gentiles, as the woman of Canaan, and that of Samaria, and the centurion, the time to admit the Greeks had not yet come. But the request was not in vain, as the word of Christ, in verses 31-32 shows, would be soon accomplished, not with speech but with the act of his passion, in his death: "Now is the judgment of this world: now shall the prince of this world be cast out. And I, if I be lifted up from the earth, will draw all men unto me. This he said, signifying what death he should die." Here we see the Kingdom of God established.

The Jews had said in response to Jesus' words here, "We have heard out of the law that Christ abides for ever: and how do you say, The Son of man must be lifted up? who is *this* Son of man?" What they had heard was the word of the prophet Daniel 7:13-14, of one whose dominion is an everlasting dominion.

> I saw in the night visions, and, behold, one like the Son of man came with the clouds of heaven, and came to the Ancient of days, and they brought him near before him. And there was given him dominion, and glory, and a

kingdom, that all people, nations, and languages, should serve him: his dominion is an everlasting dominion, which shall not pass away, and his kingdom that which shall not be destroyed.

To them this admitted of no death on the part of the Messiah. They ignored the words of the Psalmist and Zechariah the prophet. But Mark testifies of the facts of the betrayal of Christ to the death, even as foretold by the ancient prophets. He, among the followers of Christ, is alone witness to the turning of the door of betrayal. He was called into it, to take up the cross, and follow Christ to the death, which as we will see was fulfilled in other particulars. One who had given away his riches was witness to the actions of another who had sought wealth through betrayal.

11. *Another* Disciple

And Simon Peter followed Jesus, and so did another disciple: that disciple was known to the high priest, and went in with Jesus into the palace of the high priest. But Peter stood at the door without. Then went out that other disciple, which was known unto the high priest, and spoke to her that kept the door, and brought in Peter. Then said the damsel that kept the door to Peter, "Are not you also one of this man's disciples?" He said, "I am not." And the servants and officers stood there, who had made a fire of coals; for it was cold: and they warmed themselves: and Peter stood with them, and warmed himself. The high priest then asked Jesus of his disciples, and of his doctrine. Jesus answered him, "I spoke openly to the world; I ever taught in the synagogue, and in the temple, whither the Jews always resort; and in secret have I said nothing. Why do you ask me? ask them which heard me, what I have said unto them: behold, they know what I said." And when he had thus spoken, one of the officers which stood by struck Jesus with the palm of his hand, saying, "Do you answer the high priest so?" Jesus answered him, If I have spoken evil, bear witness of the evil: but if well, why do you smite me?" Now Annas had sent him bound unto Caiaphas the high priest. And Simon Peter stood and warmed himself. They said therefore to him, "Are you not also one of his disciples?" He denied it, and said, "I am not." One of the servants of the high priest, being his kinsman whose ear Peter cut off, said, "Did not I see you in the garden with him?" Peter then denied again: and immediately the cock crew.

—John 18:15-27

WE HAVE SEEN Mark is a witness to the betrayal, but here we will see he was a witness to much more. Mark and Peter render a similar account of the arraignment of Christ and Peter's denial, while Luke mentions only Peter's denial. The apostle John however brings in certain supplemental facts not given in the other gospels. He intimates the relation between Annas and Caiaphas, the name of the high priest's servant whose ear Peter had severed as being *Malchus*, and the relation of this man to another servant of the high priest, he speaks of "the damsel that kept the door," while the others mention simply "the maid," and that the fire to which they warmed themselves was made of coals. He adds more of Christ's speech before the tribunal. Now John also adds in chapter 18:15-17, "And Simon Peter followed Jesus, and so did *another disciple:* that disciple was known unto the high priest, and went in with Jesus into the palace of the high priest. But Peter stood at the door without. Then went out that other disciple, which was known unto the high priest, and spoke unto her that kept the door, and brought in Peter. Then said the damsel that kept the door to Peter, 'Are you not also one of this man's disciples?'"

John does not tell us who this disciple is, but many assume it to be John, based on the references John makes in chapter 20:2-8 regarding "the other disciple whom Jesus loved," or simply "that *other* disciple," of whom we shall examine in a later chapter. However John was not of Jerusalem, but from Galilee, it is highly unlikely he would have been known to the high priest as he had been following Jesus for three years after being called at the Jordan, having formerly been a follower of John the Baptist, and a lowly fisherman with a close brother James and a father Zebedee who kept the business going while they and their mother accompanied Jesus on his travels. They followed

ANOTHER DISCIPLE

Jesus and Jesus spent no time with the high priest. The Baptist had called the Pharisees and Saducees "a generation of vipers," so it is hardly likely his former followers would endear themselves to the high priest. Beside this we have the testimony of Acts 4:13, "Now when they saw the boldness of Peter and John, and perceived that they were unlearned and ignorant men, they marvelled; and they took knowledge of them, that they had been with Jesus." The apostle John was not recognized by Annas and Caiaphas as a familiar figure to them. Neither would the other disciples have an easy approach to the high priest, as they also were of Galilee. Also the last year had proven to be a year of mounting opposition of the priesthood and elders against Christ and his disciples. Of course this "other disciple" cannot be Judas, although being the son of Simon the Pharisee in Bethany he has a connection to the Pharisees, with whom he had plotted the arrest of Jesus, but he has ceased to be a disciple, and he would not be accompanying Peter, but rather avoiding the disciples' wrath, and taking away his silver.

This disciple must have been a new disciple of Jesus, who had formerly been familiar to the high priest and his servants. His free passage in to the palace shows he must have some eminence among the servants. He needed no introduction. Such a one could not have been a disciple of long standing with Christ. It is one newly converted or recruited into Christ's company, and as we have explained such a one is the rich young ruler, a native of Jerusalem, not a Galilaean of Galilaean speech, but one who being wealthy and religious would have welcome access to the palace of

THERE CAME ONE RUNNING

the high priest. We know from Acts 12:12 that Mark had a house in Jerusalem which he shared with Mary. This phrase "that other disciple" is identical to what we have seen in chapter 20 regarding "that other disciple," whom Jesus loved, whom we have demonstrated is Mark. Nicodemus or Joseph of Arimathea are not called the "other disciple." These righteous men would not be given notice by the plotters beforehand to a betrayal. They have no close relation to Peter in these events, in order to let him in to the palace of the high priest. We can conclude then that this "other disciple" following with Peter who went in with Jesus is in fact Mark. This shows us that when we read the account of the arraignment and denial in Mark, we must read it as the account of an eye-witness. The gospel writer himself is bearing witness to the accusations against Jesus. He is the source of the events as they happened. This explains the similarity with the accounts of Mark and Matthew. Matthew has heard it from Mark.

At the betrayal in Gethsemane Peter had just lopped the ear off the high priest's servant, Malchus, which Jesus had immediately healed. Christ then sharply told them to put the sword away. This must have confused Peter. Later Jesus would answer Pilate with, "My kingdom is not of this world: if my kingdom were of this world, then would my servants fight, that I should not be delivered to the Jews: but now is my kingdom not from hence." So Jesus is then led away bound to the palace of the high priest to be interrogated. Mark says of Jesus' disciples, "they all forsook him, and fled," and adds, in verse 51-52, "And there followed him a certain young man, having a linen cloth cast about his

ANOTHER DISCIPLE

naked body; and the young men laid hold on him: and he left the linen cloth, and fled from them naked." The "young men" had laid hold on this man in Gethsemane, as he was with Christ, and they must have borne some relation to himself, they must have known him to have singled him out particularly, one reason being the odd fact that he had lost his gorgeous clothes, having only one piece of clothing left on him.

Now although the disciples had fled from the arrest some later filtered discreetly back to the palace of the high priest to see what was happening, including an impetuous Peter, desirous of martyrdom, and this other disciple, who follow Jesus into the palace in order to see the tribunal. In Mark 14:52-53 we read, "They all forsook him and fled," and then we read of the young man fleeing away naked. Then the next verse says, "And they led Jesus away to the high priest, but Peter followed at a distance." Peter was not alone, as John reveals in John 18:15, "And Simon Peter followed Jesus, *and so did another disciple:* that disciple was known to the high priest, and went in with Jesus into the palace of the high priest." Peter followed Jesus and so did this other disciple. They had all fled, but these two, at a safe distance, double back after Jesus is led away. The relation of the naked man fleeing with the leading away of Jesus implies a connection of the man with Peter following, which John confirms.

This other disciple, however, went in *with* Jesus into the palace of the high priest. One can assume that after having fled naked from the assault of the young men, the disciples, perhaps only Peter, would have quickly supplied the naked man with some clothes. Thus dressed he would have gone back along with Peter to the house of the high priest, of whom he was known, as he had some acceptance in the palace. They already had a companionship established at the Passover feast as in John 13:23-24, "Now there was leaning on Jesus' bosom one of his disciples, whom Jesus loved. Simon Peter therefore beckoned to him, that he should ask who it should be of whom he spoke." Now Peter is for a short time left at the entrance, unable to gain access, until this disciple has a word with the maid on the door. Consider together with this that word of Christ to the rich young ruler, "Go your way, sell whatsoever you have, and give to the poor, and you shall have treasure in heaven: and come, *take up the cross*, and *follow me*;" together with, "Simon Peter *followed* Jesus and *so did another disciple*." Here it appears the young man has followed Jesus to the arraignment in the palace of the high priest.

The other disciple was familiar with the palace and its staff, he knew where to go, and it would be natural for Peter, still undeterred, to accompany such a one. The apostles would not have known this other disciple, that is, Mark, long enough to be aware of his connections with the high priest and his household, but Peter takes advantage of this connection, and is able to make his way into the high council to be a witness to the proceedings. And although the young man had lately been associated with Christ, the arrest was almost unknown to the public at this point, his relation to Christ would not have been generally known to all those in the palace. Perhaps the time in Gethsemane proved time for Peter to acquaint himself further with

ANOTHER DISCIPLE

the beloved disciple, that the man had not told Peter of the betrayal would have proved a query in Peter's mind with this man. In this manner divine providence has supplied witnesses to the trial of Christ. Without this the events recounted would have been unknown to the gospel writers. 1 John 1:3 says, "That which we have seen and heard we declare unto you."

Mark does not talk of himself, the disciple, but like Matthew's account, only of Peter, that Peter followed Christ afar off to the palace, went in and sat with the servants by the fire, as does Luke. John however introduces another element in this "other disciple." That disciple, being known to the high priest went in with Jesus to the palace of the high priest, while he says Peter stood at the door *without*, that is outside the palace door. Then he says that this other disciple, known unto the high priest speaks to her that kept the door, who happens to be the maid of the high priest, and she lets Peter in. Matthew says, "Now Peter sat without *in* the palace." It is here at the outer part of the court, inside the palace, that Peter observes what happens, "to see the end" as Matthew has it, sitting with the servants and officers warming himself at the fire.

Mark and Matthew recount the arraignment, how the chief priests and all the council sought for witness to put him to death. Luke says nothing on it, only the denial of Peter. Here we are dealing with Mark's witness, Luke the companion of Paul, has no immediate relation to these facts. But John introduces a different line, where the high priest asked Jesus of his disciples and of his doctrine. Jesus answered he "spoke openly to the world, in secret having said nothing . . . Why ask me? Ask them which heard me." Then John says Jesus is assaulted by one of the officers who strikes him with his hand, asking why he answered the high priest so. Jesus answered, "Why do you smite me?" John says he was bound, inferring he cannot defend himself. This must have been the first assault, as the other ones accounted of in Mark and Matthew are more numerous, so this dialogue in John must have come first, before the false witnesses and the general rough play Matthew and Mark recount. Many bare false witness, and their accounts did not agree, others accused him of saying he would destroy the temple that is made with hands, and in three days build one without hands, but their witness did not agree together. The high priest stood up in the midst, and asked Jesus, "Do you answer nothing?" Jesus held his peace. He then asks if he is the Christ, the Son of God. Jesus then answers, "I am," or, "you have said," and that he would see "the Son of man sitting on the right hand of power, coming on the clouds of heaven." The high priest then rends his clothes, accuses him of blasphemy and declares him guilty of death. He asks the council what they think, and they consent to the death penalty.

Matthew and Mark then speak of him being spat on, and buffeted, his face covered, others smiting him with their hands, saying "Prophesy unto us, you Christ, who smote you?" Moses had said, in Deuteronomy 18, "I will raise them up a Prophet from among their brothers, like unto you, and will put my words in his mouth; and he shall speak unto them all that I shall command him." Here then is the object of that tribunal, that is, to determine if this man were or not this Prophet—"Are

ANOTHER DISCIPLE

you the son of the blessed?" he had been asked. Moses had also said in that context, "the prophet, which shall presume to speak a word in my name, which I have not commanded him to speak, or that shall speak in the name of other gods, even that prophet shall die. And if you say in your heart, How shall we know the word which the LORD has not spoken? When a prophet speaks in the name of the LORD, if the thing follow not, nor come to pass, that is the thing which the LORD has not spoken, but the prophet has spoken it presumptuously: you shall not be afraid of him." So here they attempt what appears to be a cynical game of blind man's "prophet" with Jesus, with his face covered, as if he might show his powers, in naming the ones who smote him, and disprove his prophetic gifts, and his claim to be the Son of God, thereby incurring the death penalty. They wickedly assume him to be a sorcerer, expecting some trivial displays of power.

Matthew and Mark mention the details of Peter's three denials *after* the account of the events of Christ's arraignment, which shows us that the first denial detailed in John in verse 19 is not necessarily contingent to the events regarding Peter in verses 17-18, that is, the damsel that kept the door and her question as to whether he were a disciple, but rather an extension of that regarding the narrative about Christ in verse 15, where "Jesus went into the palace of the high priest," then verse 19, "the high priest *then* asked Jesus of his disciples and of his doctrine." John brings it in here because he is introducing this other element, the *other disciple,* and the means by which he brings Peter into the council hall. Together he gives this first denial, as it was connected with the high priest's maid who had let him in at the request of the other disciple. "Then went out that other disciple, which was known to the high priest, and spoke to her that kept the door, and brought in Peter."

John shows us that Jesus is taken to Annas the father-in-law to Caiaphas, then to Caiaphas. These two priests then reside in the same palace, around the court where all is happening. Peter and this other disciple had entered the palace, but Peter was without the central area. The other disciple had gone further in for a closer look at the proceedings as he is known to the high priest's household. This central area must have been raised some steps above the porch, adjacent to it, with various levels, and been open to view from the porch, as Jesus would soon see Peter there at his last denial— Luke says in verse 61, that later after the cock crew, "The Lord turned and looked upon Peter." But now the other disciple close in, now thinking of Peter, goes out or *beneath*, or *downwards*, as Mark puts it, to speak to the woman at the door, who happens to be the maid of the high priest, and he brings Peter in, sitting with the servants and officers around a fire of coals, to warm himself. One might ask, *downward* from where? and we would conclude from where the *writer* was standing. After the first denial Peter goes out to the porch, which was beneath or down a step or two, but still open to the inside where Luke says at this last denial, "the Lord turned and looked upon Peter and Peter remembered the word of the Lord, how he had said to him, 'Before the cock crow, you shall deny me thrice.'" The other disciple has a more intimate access to the events. It

ANOTHER DISCIPLE

reads as the account of one who was there.

Now the point of John's discourse is the relation that Christ imposes upon those disciples who heard him. "The high priest then asked Jesus of his disciples, and of his doctrine. Jesus answered him, "I spoke openly to the world; I ever taught in the synagogue, and in the temple, whither the Jews always resort; and in secret have I said nothing. Why do you ask me? ask them which heard me, what I have said to them: behold, they know what I said." This places the obligation of those of his own present in that council to speak. Now Simon Peter was there, down at the rear of the crowd with the servants, he would have heard this call of Jesus to his accusers to ask his disciples what he had taught, and this puts Peter in the spotlight, and this gives us the reason for the inquiry of the maid to Peter as to whether he were one of the disciples. It was an opportunity to Peter to declare what Christ had said, an opportunity he did not take. Matthew says a damsel says to him, "You were with Jesus of Galilee." Mark says she was a maid of the high priest. It is as if she is saying, without malice, "You were with him, you can tell us what he said and taught!" Peter then removes to the porch, and another maid accosts him there, saying to those around, "this fellow was also with Jesus of Nazareth." She says "also," as if there were another who had been taken notice of, perhaps this other disciple. Luke also mentions the two maids. John condenses the two maids into "*they* said to him, 'Are not you also one of his disciples?'" Mark writes, verses 70-71, "they that stood by said again to Peter, 'Surely you are one of them: for you are a Galilaean, and your speech agrees thereto.' But he began to curse and to swear, saying, 'I know not this man of whom you speak.'" Now if Peter's language made him suspect, we must consider that John, a candidate for this "other disciple," was also a Galilaean; if this disciple were John surely he would also be accosted by a maid for being a Galilaean, as was Peter. The "other disciple" had just spoken to the maid, in order to let Peter in, but this disciple is not accosted for his speech, and that simply because he is not a Galilaean, and is in fact known to the household and a resident of the city. He is obeyed because he is a ruler. John adds the detail which explains Peter's continuing denial in verse 26, "One of the servants of the high priest, being his kinsman whose ear Peter cut off, said, 'Did not I see you in the garden with him?'" This would make Peter fearful of retribution, or the accusation of insurrection, from this kinsman of Malchus the earless. Peter would have been surrounded by the soldiers and servants at the fire of coals, and this with Malchus' kinsman, would have proved intimidating to the bravest of souls. Peter then denied again, and immediately the cock crew. Peter's response is not simply because he is in the audience, but because he could be tried for insurrection and assault. Peter was not prepared to respond to their question, that is, what Jesus had imposed, to speak of what he had said unto them, what he had taught them.

When Jesus, after his resurrection, in the scene at the seaside, would speak with Peter regarding "the disciple whom Jesus loved," we can assume that there is now this shared experience of the "other disciple" with Peter through the events of Peter's denial before Christ and

ANOTHER DISCIPLE

those of the palace of the high priest, notwithstanding other significant shared events which we will examine in another chapter. Things have come to a bad turn for Peter and it is Mark, Peter's companion who attests to this shameful response, and we can assume that it is he who witnesses these things in his gospel at the consent or even insistence of Peter. Mark leaves out Peter's brave swordplay in the story of Malchus' severed ear, and so also mention of his kinsman, but Peter does not wish to have this information presented, preferring a self-deprecation on the events, as he is ashamed of his later actions, or perhaps it is left out as it still holds the accusation of insurrection on Peter, and best kept quiet, even though the ear was healed, at least until years later when John adds it. It does not say that any other disciples followed Jesus into the tribunal other than Peter and this other disciple, so we cannot conclude whether John was there or not. We might think of Joseph of Arimathea or Nicodemus. We know the disciples were afraid, as a few days later, after Christ's execution, it is said the doors were shut where they were assembled for fear of the Jews.

But we see a different Peter in another porch in Acts 3:11, "And as the lame man which was healed held Peter and John, all the people ran together unto them in the porch that is called Solomon's, greatly wondering." The priests, the captain of the temple, and the Sadducees came upon them and arrested them. Annas and Caiaphas and the kindred of the high priest set them in their midst, demanding an account. Christ at his tribunal had called on the high council to ask his disciples what he had taught, Peter had failed to speak up, but now this apostle speaks fearlessly about Christ, preaching the resurrection of the dead to the high priests and temple dignitaries.

This also presents us with more facts about the rich young ruler, or Mark, the other disciple—he had access to the high priest and his house, he was known to them and the servants in the palace. As a ruler he was accustomed to being fearless and authoritative, and disregarding his lessers. In calling this man as he had, Christ brought in one who would have easy access to the tribunal events, who would allow Peter to come in and be a spectator to it. Without the calling of this man there would have been no entry of Peter to the trial, and no apostolic witness to it. As we saw his surname is "Mark," which, means in the Latin, "*defence*," and here he attends the trial and makes a record of it in his gospel. Here he appears as a witness for the defendant and states his case like no other. The one whom Jesus beholding loved had become the beholder of the trial of Jesus. He presents his case, details the proceedings, the words of Christ in his defence, the lies of the false witnesses, the beatings and so forth. What John later shares of the trial are what Mark had not detailed in his gospel, yet with Peter had been a witness to, and had then told the others.

Again it is John in his gospel, years later, who enlightens us to these facts. Here we see that the young man has accompanied Jesus further than the betrayal, he went in *with* Jesus into the palace of the high priest, even as Christ had said to the rich young ruler, "come, take up the cross, and follow me." Truly John wrote, "This is the disciple which testified of these things."

12. Another Revelation of John

This is the disciple which testified of these things, and wrote these things: and we know that his testimony is true.
—*John 21:24*

THE APOSTLE JOHN was given the Revelation of Jesus Christ, and here he has also given us the revelation of *a disciple who has written a book*. As Mark has born this testimony to the betrayal of Christ, so John's concluding words also tell us:

> This is the disciple which testified of these things, and wrote these things: and we know that his testimony is true. And there are also many other things which Jesus did, the which, if they should be written every one, I suppose that even the world itself could not contain the books that should be written. Amen.

The sense of this passage, the one of whom whose testimony is true, is here associated with a book, as "books that should be written." His testimony is true, that is his book is true, and there could be many other books. This disciple who testified then is to be understood as a disciple who has written a book. Now John has just finished penning his gospel, and he closes it with this statement. He satisfies himself with what he has written as being the purpose and fullness of that he wished to convey, while alluding to another book, fully aware that there is much more that could be written, that much is to remain untold, and also some of it remained

THERE CAME ONE RUNNING

to be sought out. It is John who reveals this man to us, who unlocks his identity. Not only that but he reveals the secrets of the household of Martha and Mary, of which we will consider in a later chapter.

So here hidden in the gospels we find another story, another revelation of John, the story of the effectual calling of Mark. The one whom Jesus loved is actually the rich young man, the young ruler, he has divested himself of all his goods and property, he has joined the disciples for the Passover, become the sole confidant among the disciples of the identity of the betrayer, indeed the very fact of a betrayal, and he has witnessed this betrayal of Christ in the garden of Gethsemane, knowing it was coming. Such a one has left all to follow Christ, who in turn embraces him, and comforts him at the Passover, he alone is witness with Christ to the identity of the traitor, he is also loyal and courageous, naturally accustomed to leadership and initiative, when all the others flee he is the last to flee. He also is the witness to the trial of Christ, being familiar to the high priest's household, and is the one who enables Peter to be a fellow witness. When he writes his gospel he is the one who has seen it happen, and thus Matthew's account of the trial is derived from his, as we have no record of Matthew being there. Mark appears in the ship and on the beach as a disciple with the apostles and other disciples. "What shall this man do?" asks Peter. He has come late in to the vineyard, he has "tarried till I come," that is, till Christ had called him so late in the drama, at the eleventh hour, at the very Passover, yet early enough to follow Christ and "carry the cross," and that barely clothed. This man becomes

ANOTHER REVELATION OF JOHN

a fellow with the apostle Peter, his "son," and he writes the gospel. Christ divests him of worldly riches and gives him a rich storehouse in heaven, the rich young ruler is in heavenly treasures a rich young ruler. Here Christ gives unto this last, even as unto Peter. John says in chapter 21:24, "This is the disciple which testified of these things, and wrote these things: and we know that his testimony is true." John and the other apostles know that this man's testimony is true. This disciple wrote these things, such a writer as would pen a gospel is meant, and that is Mark. Here we have the apostolic corroboration of the evangelist Mark, inasmuch as the same way as Peter would confirm the writings of Paul. He leaves house, brothers, family, lands, for Christ's sake, and the gospel's, but he receives an hundredfold now in this time, houses, and brothers, and sisters, and mothers, and children, and lands, with persecutions and in the world to come eternal life. As a companion to Peter and Paul he would share the persecutions of Nero in the empire's Babylon, Rome.

Christ's "doing what he will" shows in the events of this story. The disciples quibbling over position, the appointments of ones called late to certain roles, like Matthew and Mark, the words to Peter, "What is that to you? take what is yours and go your way." The admission of the children despite their being held back by the disciples, the coming of the young man, and the healing of the blind man, the confiding of significant details to the one whom Jesus loved, one who had only just entered into the band, the holding back of those from the apostles—Christ is always central, all happens around him, he overrides, and receives and orders, outsiders come in while insiders are cast out or are chastised for their inconstancy, despite the desires of the inner circle.

Paul shared a similar story to that of the young man, in that he shared a covetous nature, a position and status among the wealthy and religious rulers, with its attendant education, who had also come to Christ outside of the circle of the disciples, and despite them had come into their company through the confirming recognition of James, Cephas and John in regard to Christ's personal stamp and calling upon him. These had learned that the first were last and the last first, that Christ was among them as one that did serve, as they had learned at the supper in the washing of the feet. So Christ does what he wills with his own, who come to him despite the stern discouragement and fear of other Christian brothers. This parable and the example of Mark's calling would have set a precedent for recognizing that of Paul's.

Mark hides his story in the gospel for the same reason as Peter's desire for self-effacement in it, the avoiding of recounting the things that would promote his own glory. It is as the Proverb 27:2, "Let another man praise you, and not your own mouth." The giving away all one has and the following of Christ so closely to the cross could not be allowed to stand as a mark of renown for the gospel writer, but it was to be even as John the Baptist's intent, "*He* must increase but I must decrease." This self effacing is present in the presentation of his gospel as it regards Peter also. As Godet wrote, "Peter omits what holds to his favour and admits only those which tend to his humiliation." Mark removes the "certain ruler" found

ANOTHER REVELATION OF JOHN

in Luke, referring to him simply as "one running." It is to be left for another, years later, the apostle John himself, to bear witness to this disciple, as "the one who testified to these things." Even so, the identity of this disciple, this witness, enigmatically disclosed as it is, has been hid for centuries.

This also has implications for our understanding of John, who has always been cast into this role of "the one whom Jesus loved." We have always seen this aspect of him as a doddery lovable old coot, one who fondly gives himself this moniker. But if we consider this conclusion at face value it is almost an elitist boast, as if he were the favourite, a sentiment actually foreign to him, to the equitable nature of a twin, foreign to the lesson of the parable of the labourers, and alien to the spirit of the proverb, "let another man praise you." His whole aim is for *others* to know they are beloved, "that we might believe on the name of the Son of God, and know we have eternal life," and not to boast that he is the favourite. This idea has coloured our view of John as gospel writer and recipient of the Revelation and has influenced the way we see his epistles. Paintings of the Last Supper have always shown a young beardless John resting on Jesus' bosom, a gentle, almost feminine personality. It does not sit with the nickname "son of thunder" at all, and neither with his calling as the Seer of the Apocalypse. It is a culturally and historically ingrained image hard to divorce from him, yet incongruous with the personality of this fierce fisherman. What would sit better to oppose the heathen world power from Patmos with a message of Christ's wrath and rule—a strong thunderous figure, whose brother James had gone to martyrdom for opposing King Herod, or a beardless weak youth always in need of a cuddle?

Then Christ's embrace of this man also has a context, not that of a favoured embrace as to a child, or a boyfriend with its questionable connotations, but an appropriate consolation to a strong brave personality, one lately weakened and chastened by the conflict of distancing oneself from godless acquaintances and riches and family members, Christ is giving a needed strengthening to one who would also soon go to the cross in the events of the terrible betrayal played out at Gethsemane, an embracing in his warm robe to one come almost naked out of the cold night. Here on the night of the Passover this young man has left, or even been cast out from, the family in which he had always shared the annual Passover feast, that great feast of the Hebrew family groups, celebrated in their own houses, the blood on the lintel, he has left this familiar house, with its brothers, sisters, father, mother, which since his birth has been his annual custom of observing with his family, and so has joined with Jesus and the disciples. He has divested himself of virtually all his threads to go through the eye of the needle, and now rests in the seamless robe of Christ. The Eucharist then is thus made a place of comfort and consolation for past trials, and a strengthening for yet future, even imminent ones, and a partaking of the promised eternal life. As Christ said, in John 6:54, "Whoso eats my flesh, and drinks my blood, has eternal life; and I will raise him up at the last day."

13. Woman, Behold Your Son

He said unto his mother: Woman, behold, your son. And he said to that disciple: "Behold, your mother." And from that hour, the disciple took her near himself.
—*John 19:26-27*

And when he had considered the thing, he came to the house of Mary the mother of John, whose surname was Mark; where many were gathered together praying ~ And Barnabas and Saul returned from Jerusalem, when they had fulfilled their ministry, and took with them John, whose surname was Mark ~ So they, being sent forth by the Holy Ghost, departed to Seleucia; and from there they sailed to Cyprus. And when they were at Salamis, they preached the word of God in the synagogues of the Jews: and they had also John to their minister. ~ Now when Paul and his company loosed from Paphos, they came to Perga in Pamphylia: and John departing from them returned to Jerusalem. ~ And some days after Paul said unto Barnabas, "Let us go again and visit our brothers in every city where we have preached the word of the Lord, and see how they do." And Barnabas determined to take with them John, whose surname was Mark. But Paul thought not good to take him with them, who departed from them from Pamphylia, and went not with them to the work. And the contention was so sharp between them, that they departed asunder one from the other: and so Barnabas took Mark, and sailed unto Cyprus.
—*Acts 12:12, 25, 13:4-5, 13, 15:36-39*

As JOHN'S GOSPEL has enlightened us to certain facts regarding Mark, these facts open up the door to more elsewhere, like dominoes. In John's account of the crucifixion in chapter nineteen we read of Christ's seamless coat being taken by the soldiers. Here again, as in the account of the linen cloth, we have an account of clothing, as with the naked man losing his linen cloth, Christ himself gives away everything, his life and his raiment being taken from him. Modest discretion has rightly covered him with a cloth in our crucifixes, icons and paintings, but he was stark naked on that cross. The type as figured in the naked young man now proceeds to the true. The garments were parted into four parts, and lots were cast for the coat, which consisted of a single strand woven into one vesture, without seam. Now immediately after this episode, we have the account where Jesus, nailed to the tree, sees his mother, and his mother's sister, Mary the wife of Cleophas, where we have these words:

> Now there stood by the cross of Jesus his mother, and his mother's sister, Mary the wife of Cleophas, and Mary Magdalene. When Jesus therefore saw his mother, and the disciple standing by, whom he loved, he said to his mother, "Woman, behold your son!" Then said he to the disciple, "Behold your mother!" And from that hour that disciple took her unto his own home.

Here once more we have an appearance of "the disciple whom he loved," here standing by the cross as Christ is dying. Of course the assumption has always been that John was the beloved disciple, and that he was entrusted with the care of Christ's mother Mary. John no doubt would be present, but again as we have concluded, this particular disciple is not John but the young man, Mark. Here in fact *Mark* is the one "standing by." Here he has been faithful to Christ's word to him, "take up the cross and follow me." He now stands at the cross with Jesus' mother and the others.

After Peter's miraculous release from prison in Jerusalem by the angel, we read in Acts 12:12, "And when he had considered the thing, he came to the house of Mary the mother of John, whose surname was Mark; where many were gathered together praying." John is the Hebrew name, Mark is the Latin. Here we have some facts. That is, Mary is the mother of John, and that this John is surnamed Mark. This agrees with Jesus' saying to his mother, "Woman behold your son," and the "Behold your mother," to the disciple whom he loved. The charge from the cross and this verse in Acts meet thus on two points. This also agrees with Christ's words:

> Truly I say unto you, There is no man that has left house, or brothers, or sisters, or father, or *mother,* or wife, or children, or lands, for my sake, and the gospel's, But he shall receive an hundredfold now in this time, houses, and brothers, and sisters, and *mothers*, and children, and lands, with persecutions; and in the world to come eternal life.

Mark receives a mother in Christ's mother, whom the disciple would take into his home, even Christ's own mother, the blessed Virgin. Such is the depth of love that Christ has for this young man that he should entrust them both to each other in a familial relation. It is evident in this context that he later receives a house, one to which is also "the house of Mary, the mother of John." The charge to Peter to feed his lambs would also bring him into the circle of this relation with Mark. Here one who has written a gospel, who has left all for it, finds a mother in Mary, and a father in Peter.

Peter, after his imprisonment ordeal, naturally goes to the home of Mark, in the city, that is, his nearest and dearest adoptive son, and the residence of the Virgin Mary, the mother of Jesus. Peter, in assuring them of his safety and deliverance, not willing to expose them to the charge of harbouring an escapee, in verse 17, then goes to another undisclosed location. King Herod, the one who had imprisoned him, and had already killed James, the brother of John the apostle, 12:2, is then said to have removed from Jerusalem to Caesarea, verse 19, and there to have in time died for his blasphemy, verse 23-25: "And immediately the angel of the Lord smote him, because he gave not God the glory: and he was eaten of worms, and gave up the ghost." It then follows with, "But the word of God grew and multiplied. And Barnabas and Saul returned from Jerusalem, when they had fulfilled their ministry, and took with them John, whose surname was *Mark*."

Peter, after the death of the tyrant, would then have had the freedom to be at large, and the gospel continued to spread, with Barnabas and Saul departing to Antioch, as the persecution had passed. Mark, then, went with Barnabas and Saul, as recounted in Acts chapter 13, where he would play a critical role in the very first missionary journey to Cyprus. He would be a major asset as he is the one who testified to the betrayer at the Supper, and is an eye witness to the death and resurrection of Christ. He would, along with Barnabas and Paul, testify to the Jews in the synagogue, the false teacher Elymas, and the Roman governor of the island. Barnabas, being of Cyprus, knew the island, and would have invaluable insight and contacts on bringing the gospel there.

In Antioch they are separated to the work given

them by the Holy Spirit, and sail to Salamis in Cyprus via Seleucia, preaching in the synagogue, with John as their minister. Here they confront Elymas the sorcerer, and the deputy Sergius Paulus is converted, in verse 12, while in verse 13 we have Saul directly called Paul for the first time. This conversion of Sergius begins the fulfilling of Christ's word regarding Paul at his conversion, in Acts 9:15, "for he is a chosen vessel unto me, to bear my name before the Gentiles, and kings, and the children of Israel." The conversion of the governor Paulus here coincides with Saul receiving a Latin name, Paul, which means *little*. When they depart from Cyprus, Mark leaves them at Pamphylia on the mainland in order to return to Jerusalem. "Barnabas and Saul" then preached the gospel on an extended mission trip from Antioch to Iconium, Lystra and Derbe, and then return, as "Paul and Barnabas," Paul now having the primacy in the team. Some time after this Paul determined to revisit the cities to see how they fared, and we have this statement regarding Mark:

And some days after Paul said unto Barnabas, "Let us go again and visit our brothers in every city where we have preached the word of the Lord, and see how they do." And Barnabas determined to take with them John, whose surname was Mark. But Paul thought not good to take him with them, who departed from them from Pamphylia, and went not with them to the work. And the contention was so sharp between them, that they departed asunder one from the other: and so Barnabas took Mark, and sailed to Cyprus; And Paul chose Silas, and departed, being recommended by the brothers unto the grace of God.

It was appropriate that Mark sails with Barnabas to Cyprus, as that was the scene of his previous travels.

THERE CAME ONE RUNNING

In 2 Timothy 4:9-11 we read Paul, writing to Timothy,

> Do your diligence to come shortly to me: For Demas has forsaken me, having loved this present world, and is departed to Thessalonica; Crescens to Galatia, Titus to Dalmatia. Only Luke is with me. Take Mark, and bring him with you: for he is profitable to me for the ministry.

Paul appears to have smarted at the decision of Mark to return to Jerusalem, Acts 15:38, "But Paul thought not good to take him with them, who departed from them from Pamphylia, and went not with them to the work." Given Mark's unique witness to the Passion events, it is rather sad that Paul's new converts would not have the opportunity of hearing Mark, and this shows the strength of Paul's objection to him not coming with them to the work. But later he appears to have changed his attitude, and values his ministry—"he is profitable to me."

Now we can ascertain further details regarding Barnabas and so also Mark. In Acts 4:36, *Joses* was surnamed *Barnabas*, "the son of consolation," he was a Levite, and of the country of Cyprus. In Mark 6:3 we are told that *Joses* is the brother of Jesus.

> "Is not this the carpenter, the son of Mary, the brother (cousin) of James, and Joses, and of Juda, and Simon? and are not his sisters here with us?" And they were offended at him.

In Matthew 27:56 we learn that he is the son of Mary, the sister of the mother of Jesus.

> And many women were there beholding afar off, which followed Jesus from Galilee, ministering unto him: Among which was Mary Magdalene, and Mary the mother of James and Joses, and the mother of Zebedee's children.

This is explained by the fact that in scripture, "brother" or "sister" is a synonym for "cousin." So Jesus' brothers are actually cousins, that is "James, Joses, Juda and Simon." Perhaps Mary was cousin to the virgin, as she bears the same name. We have Joses and we have his brother James, who was an apostle, called James the less, as opposed to James the greater who had, with John, Zebedee to their father. This James the less had *Alphaeus* or *Cleophas* for his father, who was married to a Mary who was the sister of the virgin Mary. Alphaeus was also the father of *Levi*, that is *Matthew*, the publican, or tax collector. So, if it be the one and the same Alphaeus, Barnabas was related to Christ as a cousin, and brother to Matthew, the apostle and evangelist. One could suppose the Simon to be Simon the Zealot or Canaanite, another apostle. We will examine all this in the chapter on the Lord's brothers. Judas is the *Jude* of the epistle, which given its sharing a name notorious with the betrayer, is singularly devoted to the subject of apostates and false teachers.

Simeon the prophet had been told by God that he would not see death until he had seen "the consolation of Israel," that is Christ, when he saw the baby Jesus. So here Barnabas is called "the son of consolation," in a relation to the Messiah, but also Christlike in spirit, as if to the Father.

Much later Mark would be found in Colossae, along with Luke, in the letter to Philemon, verse 24, "There you salute Epaphras, my fellowprisoner in Christ Jesus; Marcus, Aristarchus, Demas, Lucas, my fellow labourers." We read in Colossians 4:10, where Paul asks that hospitality be showed to Marcus:

THERE CAME ONE RUNNING

> Aristarchus my fellowprisoner salutes you, and Marcus, sister's son to Barnabas, (touching whom you received commandments: if he come to you, receive him;)

Here intimated to us is that Marcus "is sister's son to Barnabas." So Marcus is related to Barnabas, who is in fact his uncle. As Barnabas is cousin, or brother to Jesus, as Joses, so Mark is of the family of Jesus. This explains the entrusting of his mother to Mark, as he is in fact related. He stands by the cross with Mary his grandmother, his mother is not there, unless her name was Joanna the wife of Chuza, Herod's steward, or Susannah, who were known to have ministered to Christ of their substance, being wealthy women, Luke 8:3, but this seems unlikely. In that Christ gives him a mother in Mary indicates that his own mother had already died. Mark came of a wealthy family, but the name of his birth mother cannot be proven. It is likely he is a Levite, as Barnabas is a Levite, hence of the city, Jerusalem being a Levitical city. He had a family home in the city, as shown in the episode of Peter's imprisonment. Also the mother of Zebedee's children stood there. So it is that we have these strong blood ties among the apostles.

As to why Mark returned and did not proceed with Barnabas and Paul we can make charitable suppositions. We know he does not lack courage. It cannot have been through fear that he declined. He has the care of Christ's mother, Mary. He has been entrusted by Christ to Peter, not Paul, and would naturally wish to be of service to that apostle, his father in the faith. He may well have felt keenly Christ's charge to him regarding his adoptive mother, and

WOMAN, BEHOLD YOUR SON

honour due to his adoptive father, and that due regard could not be paid to Paul's authority in the matter. "Honour your father" is something he had observed from his youth, and he would not have refused his duty to that injunction, toward Peter, and particularly as it involved Christ's mother, and the passing of that role upon him by the Son of God himself, and given the familial connections it was natural that Christ would devolve these relations upon him and his mother. The missionary journey into Cyprus was a departure from these relations that were so divinely laid upon this young man, who would have felt keenly the need to carry the gospel to his uncle's island. To have continued further as the others did would entail a greater period of time away from these concerns. Mark was a follower, not a leader, he would have gone to Cyprus in respect to and out of his relation to Barnabas. Paul would not have understood all this easily, perhaps he was unaware of all the facts, given Mark's self-effacing nature. Curiously after this departure from Barnabas, Paul would find Timothy at Lystra, who in his first letter is addressed as, "Timothy, my *own* son in the faith." Thus Peter and Paul have their sons.

Here we observe that there is a strong familial trend in the ranks of the apostles. This would explain something of the cohesion and loyalty given Christ during the tough times, when "many of his disciples went back, and walked no more with him. Then said Jesus unto the twelve, Will you also go away?" Blood ties are the strongest. Much of the gospel story then is tied in to the family of Christ, of which we shall

THERE CAME ONE RUNNING

examine in a later chapter. We see this when after the resurrection Jesus says in John 20:17 to Mary Magdalene, "go to my *brothers*, and say to them, I ascend unto my Father, and your Father; and to my God, and your God."

14. The *Other* Disciple

The first day of the week comes Mary Magdalene early, when it was yet dark, unto the sepulchre, and sees the stone taken away from the sepulchre. Then she runs, and comes to Simon Peter, and to the other disciple, whom Jesus loved, and says to them, "They have taken away the Lord out of the sepulchre, and we know not where they have laid him." Peter therefore went forth, and that other disciple, and came to the sepulchre. So they ran both together: and the other disciple did outrun Peter, and came first to the sepulchre. And he stooping down, and looking in, saw the linen clothes lying; yet went he not in. Then comes Simon Peter following him, and went into the sepulchre, and sees the linen clothes lie, and the napkin, that was about his head, not lying with the linen clothes, but wrapped together in a place by itself. Then went in also that other disciple, which came first to the sepulchre, and he saw, and believed. For as yet they knew not the scripture, that he must rise again from the dead. Then the disciples went away again to their own home.
—*John 20:1-10*

IF WE ARE to be consistent with this assertion regarding "the one whom Jesus loved" we must carry it through on all points, and this leads us to yet another startling conclusion to this portion of the narrative in the gospel of John, in the examination of the empty tomb by Peter and "the disciple whom Jesus loved."

We have always assumed that it was Peter and *John*, the writer of the gospel, as we have heard in all our fond Easter accounts, running to the sepulchre. But if we are correct in assuming the identity of this beloved disciple as being *Mark*, then it was not John, the gospel writer running with Peter to the sepulchre, but Mark the evangelist. If it was John one might expect also James, his inseparable twin brother, to be in the picture as well, but this is not the case.

Peter and "that other disciple," having heard the report of the empty tomb from Mary Magdalene, who too was running, went forth and came to the sepulchre. Peter and this other disciple ran both together, and "the other disciple did outrun Peter." Then having arrived first this disciple waited, as Peter went in. Why is it that it is important to describe this "running" to the sepulchre? And why does this disciple *wait* for Peter to enter before he goes in? The young man who came to Christ, the "one whom Jesus beholding loved" was described as "there came one running," by Mark in 10:17. Here the one came running did "*outrun* Peter" to the outside of the tomb. A younger man, such as Mark, would run faster than an older one, a sailor—was he bowlegged?—as Peter was. It also says regarding Peter's colleague, "And he stooping down, and looking in, sees the linen clothes lying, yet went he not in." Here we have a reference to *linen clothing*, set aside, much like the certain young man, as recounted in Mark's gospel, who "followed him, having a linen cloth cast about his naked body; and the young men laid hold on him: and he left the linen cloth and fled away naked." Here the young man observes this cloth. He sees the napkin that wrapped Christ's head laid aside separately. He is struck by the riddle of this scene, no body, only clothing, in the tomb. Perhaps he finds it resonates with his own experience of having fled naked, of having given away all he had, and then being comforted by

THE OTHER DISCIPLE

Christ at the Passover. Peter enters the sepulchre. The man had been told by Christ, "take up your cross and follow me." This other disciple *then* goes in, he follows Christ in to the very tomb, *after* Peter, and there the penny drops, it is stated that *he believed,* that is, he believed that Christ had risen from the dead. Christ has risen from the dead, naked, having given away all he had, including his grave clothes. For Christ the threads have not gone through the eye, they cannot, as the scripture says, "Naked came I out of my mother's womb, and naked shall I return there." Here is the first account of someone believing the resurrection. Here the one who has been invited to follow Jesus follows him even further into the tomb. In this the last has become the first. Yet this disciple, having run ahead, does not enter into the tomb at first, but *waits* for Peter to do so. John would not have felt to have to defer to Peter but would have gone straight in, as they were equals, but if it is Mark, this explains the deference given to Peter in allowing him to enter in to the sepulchre first, as he is the follower of the apostle. Here this agrees with the young ruler's following the commandments from his youth, in that he defers in honour to the elder, the superior, to enter into that holy place. Again we have in the running, one who came first, who defers to the one who came last, that is Peter, so that the last became the first, in entering the sepulchre.

These disciples are then said to return "to their own home;" it says *home*, as if they resided in the same place, most likely Mark's family home, which, given the later companionship of Peter and Mark, would infer that Peter had already taken him under his wing, as would be confirmed soon in the appearance and meal on the beach with Christ, where Peter is concerned with the future of "the one whom Jesus loved," displayed in his question, "What shall this man do?" We observed in the escaping from the prison Peter goes to the "house of Mary the mother of John, whose surname was Mark." Peter and Mark then, after Christ's death have a paternal friendship in Mary's house. This relation then, beginning with the Lord's supper, the events of the betrayal, and trial, and the resurrection then leads to the events of the beach, where the young man follows Jesus and Peter, and Peter now can ask his questions of the Lord regarding him, a young man who has now shared his house with Peter.

It says that "as yet, they knew not the scripture, that he must rise again from the dead." Much later, in Acts chapter two we have an idea of what this verse is, Peter preaches to the crowd at Pentecost regarding this scene in the tomb and in Acts 2:30-32 he quotes the scripture from King David, Psalm 16:10:

> Therefore being a prophet, and knowing that God had sworn with an oath to him, that of the fruit of his loins, according to the flesh, he would raise up Christ to sit on his throne; He seeing this before spoke of the resurrection of Christ, that his soul was not left in hell, neither his flesh did see corruption. This Jesus has God raised up, whereof we all are witnesses.

So here in the account of the empty tomb we have another story that resonates with psychological observations, that connects with the story of Mark.

Mark, the writer of the gospel recounts Christ's words to the young man as thus, in Mark 10:21, "Then

Jesus beholding him loved him, and said unto him, One thing you lack: go your way, sell whatsoever you have, and give to the poor, and you shall have treasure in heaven: and come, take up the cross, and follow me." See how these words have been borne out in this account—he has given away what he had, even to his clothing, he has taken up the cross, has been an intimate, even a unique witness, the first witness to the betrayal of Christ, has stood at the very cross at the death of Jesus, now he still follows Christ in to his tomb, and is among the first to witness the resurrection, indeed, with the women, the first to believe it. He sees the linen. What Christ had demanded of the man, in giving away all he had, he had done also and more-so, in giving away all he had, even to the shame of a public and naked death, an execution. Now the other question asked by the man, regarding the eternal life, "What must I do to find eternal life?" finds its marvellous fulfilment in the absence of Christ's body and the presence of the grave clothes laid neatly aside. "He is not here, but is risen," the angel had spoken to Mary Magdalene, Joanna, and Mary the mother of James, so the young man now has "treasure in heaven," this Jesus has God raised up. The one come running, the young ruler, was invited by Christ to come, and here he follows, running, even further in, "Come, take up the cross and follow me." And here he is, he saw and believed. God would raise up Christ to sit on his throne, and here a rich young ruler has given away all his goods and earthly status, has followed Christ in order to bear witness to his resurrection from the grave to heaven.

15. Let Him Be As The Younger

And there was also a strife among them, which of them should be accounted the greatest. And he said to them, "The kings of the Gentiles exercise lordship over them; and they that exercise authority upon them are called benefactors. But you shall not be so: but he that is greatest among you, let him be as the younger; and he that is chief, as he that does serve. For whether is greater, he that sits at meat, or he that serves? is not he that sits at meat? but I am among you as he that serves. You are they which have continued with me in my temptations. And I appoint unto you a kingdom, as my Father has appointed unto me; that you may eat and drink at my table in my kingdom, and sit on thrones judging the twelve tribes of Israel."
—*Luke 22:24-30*

IN MARK CHAPTER nine, the disciples, on the road to Jerusalem, had argued among themselves who should be the greatest. In verses 35-37 Christ asked them about it, "but they held their peace, and he said, If any man desire to be first, the same shall be last of all, and servant of all. And he took a child, and set him in the midst of them: and when he had taken him in his arms, he said to them, Whosoever shall receive one of such children in my name, receives me: and whosoever shall receive me, receives not me, but him that sent me." He then spoke of offences, "Whosoever should offend these little ones that believe in me, it were better a millstone hung round their necks and cast into the sea." If your hand, foot or eye offend you, "cut it off," "pluck it out." "Have salt in yourselves and have peace with one another," he concludes. After this we have the events of chapter ten, including the calling of the rich young ruler. In our text, Luke, in chapter 22:24, writes of the same thing, but in the context of the Lord's supper, "And there was also a strife among them, which of them should be accounted the greatest."

Here in this book we have seen that Christ, in the face of his arguing ambitious apostles, confounded all by choosing a young man, barely a child, and brought him in to their midst to play a key role in the witnessing the events surrounding his betrayal, death and resurrection. Jesus said to them, "All you shall be offended because of me this night: for it is written, I will smite the shepherd, and the sheep shall be scattered." Yet in face of this ancient word Peter and all the disciples had boasted their loyalty, that they would die with Christ and not deny him. Peter vainly declared, "Lord, I am ready to go with you, both into prison, and to death." Jesus had quoted the prophet, but here they did not believe the prophecy. Then at the betrayal, the hour and the power of darkness, all the disciples forsook him, and fled as Christ and the prophet had foretold.

In Mark chapter nine not long before the calling of the young man, Peter, with James and John had seen the glory, Christ in majesty with Moses and Elijah in the holy mount. In light of this the smiting the shepherd and scattering of the sheep seemed incongruent to the glory to come. But Peter later wisely said "We have also a more sure word of prophecy; whereunto you do well that you take heed." So they fled in fear, giving the lie to their claim to be the greatest. However as we have seen the naked young man tarried last, when the others had fled he was still on the scene, and was the last to flee, indeed he was, with Peter to venture into the lion's den, the court of the high priest, unscathed, without the scandal of a denial.

In our text, Luke 22:24-29, we see Christ's answer to the strife at the Passover. We read of kings, lords and benefactors among the Gentiles. It is not to be so among the Christians, he that is greatest is as the younger, the chief among them as the one who serves.

The young man was the young ruler, he was used to the idea of exercising lordship or authority, of being the chief. His life was one of preparedness for that role in society, he was one who sat at meat. But he had come in to a society where others had spent time with Christ, in his temptations, or trials. These were to sit at his table in his kingdom, on thrones judging the twelve tribes of Israel. They were appointed a kingdom, but here they are taking their place at Christ's table in that upper room, squabbling about position, as if they were to take the mantle of the rich ruler. Here Jesus brings in one who has been stripped of these notions, even all his possessions, into their midst. It is in this context that Jesus washes the disciples' feet. John describes this washing, John 13:3-17:

Jesus knowing that the Father had given all things into his hands, and that he was come from God, and went to God; He rises from supper, and laid aside his garments; and took a towel, and girded himself. After that he pours water into a basin, and began to wash the disciples' feet, and to wipe them with the towel wherewith he was girded. Then he comes to Simon Peter: and Peter says to him, "Lord, do you wash my feet?" Jesus answered and said to him, "What I do you

LET HIM BE AS THE YOUNGER

know not now; but you shall know hereafter." Peter said to him, "You shall never wash my feet." Jesus answered him, "If I wash you not, you have no part with me." Simon Peter said to him, "Lord, not my feet only, but also my hands and my head." Jesus said to him, "He that is washed needs not save to wash his feet, but is clean every whit: and you are clean, but not all." For he knew who should betray him; therefore he said, "You are not all clean." So after he had washed their feet, and had taken his garments, and was set down again, he said to them, "Do you know what I have done to you? You call me Master and Lord: and you say well; for so I am. If I then, your Lord and Master, have washed your feet; you also ought to wash one another's feet. For I have given you an example, that you should do as I have done to you. Truly, Truly, I say unto you, The servant is not greater than his lord; neither he that is sent greater than he that sent him. If you know these things, happy are you if you do them."

The disciples had refused to volunteer to wash the others feet, seeing it as a menial chore, beneath the dignity of "the greatest." The Lord Jesus responds, not with words, but actions, by taking the menial chore himself. This is how we are to understand this action of the washing of the feet, the childish squabbling over position and status, which had invaded the holy feast of Passover, a Passover that was to be subsumed into the Lord's Supper in the initiating of the New Covenant. No wonder Jesus is dead serious, the kingdom of God starts with the apostles, and it is this humility they must understand. Peter responds in surprise, "You shall never wash my feet!" But Jesus answered him, "If I do not wash you, you have no part with me." Then Peter overcompensates, "Lord, not my feet only, but also my hands and my head." Not amused, Jesus keeps to the point in teaching Peter, "He that is washed needs not

THERE CAME ONE RUNNING

save to wash his feet, but is clean every whit: and you are clean, but not all. For he knew who should betray him; therefore said he, You are not all clean."

Now the young man was present in that room and was witness to these events, even to the identity of the one who was not clean, who would betray Christ. When Jesus said "he that is greatest among you let him be as the younger," the "younger" among this group was the disciple leaning on his bosom, whom Jesus loved. Here was a young man who had only just given away all his wealth as if it meant nothing, he had given away his status, his greatness in being a ruler, and had come barely dressed in an abject shivering humility in to the upper room, he was the antithesis to their hollow claims to greatness, he is the epitome of the childlikeness Jesus loves and desires in his own. Earlier on the road, in Mark chapter nine, Christ spoke of that familiar saying that we saw in the parable of the labourers and in the forsaking of family for the gospel, there associated with the difficulty of the rich entering the kingdom, that is, "If any man desire to be first, the same shall be last of all, and servant of all," and here he has placed this word in the context of *a child*.

> But they held their peace: for by the way they had disputed among themselves, who should be the greatest. And he sat down, and called the twelve, and said to them, "If any man desire to be first, the same shall be last of all, and servant of all." And he took a child, and set him in the midst of them: and when he had taken him in his arms, he said to them, "Whosoever shall receive one of such children in my name, receives me: and whosoever shall receive me, receives not me, but him that sent me."

And as he then by way of an object lesson had

LET HIM BE AS THE YOUNGER

set a child before them, he now places before them a young man, he receives this man in the Passover scene, cold from lack of clothing, in his arms, warming him with his cloak. This was more than object lesson but example. He had said "whosoever receives one of such children in my name receives me," and not just to receive himself but him that sent him, that is the Father. In course of events he would make Peter a father to this young man, where fatherhood and brotherhood would transcend wealth and status and position, where Peter's concern was not for greatness but feeding the lambs. "He that is greatest among you let him be as the younger" is the sum of the admonition. The young man had performed acts of service in selling what he had and giving the money to the poor, Jesus had said he that is chief be as he that does serve, and "whether is greater, he that sits at meat, or he that serves? is not he that sits at meat? but I am among you as he that serves." He washes their feet, and he brings in a child, a young chief, a ruler, one that sits at meat, to serve and be an example for the apostles. Peter, later, in accompanying the young disciple in to the trial at the high priest's palace, was fulfilling this word, perhaps consciously he is taking it to heart, for he is following the lead or example of this young man, he is being as the younger, the younger follows Christ to the palace of the high priest, so does Peter, the younger lets Peter in.

Christ does not merely talk in teaching, but he acts. Here he has orchestrated an example of the humility he desires in the calling of the young man, that serves to instruct the apostles, and illustrates in the highest manner his teaching. As Mark chapter nine speaks of

THERE CAME ONE RUNNING

this child so Luke 9:48 adds, "for he that is least among you all, the same shall be great." Yet the greatness of this younger has been veiled, hidden, it is in his leastness that he is great, which shows in his obscure, even hidden position in the narrative. The story, as we have uncovered it, is truly a remarkable thing in that it shows the greatness of Christ as he orchestrates people and events in a seemingly casual effortless manner, the stars in their courses seem to orbit about him, where all things are harnessed into the arc of His almighty will.

16. A Mask Removed

Hofmann's picture of Christ and the young man, reproduced on the cover of this book, captures that moment the scripture describes: "Jesus beholding him loved him." It also captures the man in his pride, as one brought up with wealth and status, garbed in rich clothing. We see his back toward us, his hand appears to rest proud and rigid on his hip, as if he would walk away from the call and the love expressed toward him. It does not convey the inner desperation of the man, that drives him to seek Christ. Here we see a mask, a toughness, a stout face, that displays the wealthy and the self-sufficient, who remain indecisive under that challenge Christ poses for the rich, it is harder for a camel—or a rope, to go through the eye of a needle. But that which is impossible with men is possible with God. This mask that has covered this man in the gospels, that has raised the question of his fate, we have here pulled aside, the young man has shown his face to us, he is found stripped bare.

What we lose in our assumption of John as the beloved disciple at the Passover, the trial, the cross and the resurrection we gain in that of another disciple, that is Mark, with a hidden story that shows the glory and power of the Lord Christ, and it is John himself who reveals all this to us. What we have assumed to be the facts was in consequence of our not holding to the veracity of the very words of scripture we have roughly fashioned to our assumptions. Here we see something extraordinary in this hidden story that enlightens us to the Passion of Christ with new insight and understanding. To enter into the kingdom of God the man had to thread the needle. In doing this, in giving away all he had, all his threads, his status and wealth, he was, in consequence led into the very Passion story—the Eucharist, the betrayal, the trial, the death on the cross, and finally the resurrection of Jesus. In this he inherits mothers and fathers and brothers, and eternal life. Thus he enters into the kingdom of God and he bears witness to it all in his gospel. With God all things are possible. This remarkable, extraordinary story unveiled to us serves as a model, a template to our faith. He saw and believed, and so do we.

The words of Christ from Mark 10:25-31 then, are a prophecy quick of fulfilment, a paean to those of the rich who would come and cast off their old life to follow Christ for treasures in heaven, presenting a view of the implacable will of Christ among his disciples, his chosen ones. Here we have an illustration of those who would give up house, brothers, sisters, father, mother, or wife, or children, or lands for Christ's sake and the gospel's, who shall receive an hundredfold now in this time, houses, and brothers, and sisters, and mothers, and children, and lands, with persecutions, and in the world to come eternal life. But many that are first shall be last; and the last first. We have then in the account of the rich young ruler the conversion and calling of a significant member among the apostles, the evangelist Mark.

17. Mary Magdalene and Bethany

After two days was the feast of the Passover, and of unleavened bread: and the chief priests and the scribes sought how they might take him by craft, and put him to death. But they said, Not on the feast day, lest there be an uproar of the people. And being in Bethany in the house of Simon the leper, as he sat at meat, there came a woman having an alabaster box of ointment of spikenard very precious; and she brake the box, and poured it on his head. And there were some that had indignation within themselves, and said, "Why was this waste of the ointment made? For it might have been sold for more than three hundred pence, and have been given to the poor." And they murmured against her. And Jesus said, "Let her alone; why do you trouble her? she has wrought a good work on me. For you have the poor with you always, and whensoever you will you may do them good: but me you have not always. She has done what she could: she is come aforehand to anoint my body to the burying. Truly I say unto you, Wheresoever this gospel shall be preached throughout the whole world, this also that she has done shall be spoken of for a memorial of her." And Judas Iscariot, one of the twelve, went unto the chief priests, to betray him unto them. And when they heard it, they were glad, and promised to give him money. And he sought how he might conveniently betray him.
—*Mark 14:1-11*

HERE IN THIS supplemental chapter we have another gospel story hidden in the narrative, that of the house of Mary and Martha at Bethany, where the raising of Lazarus took place.

The gospel writers present certain facts to us. They

complement one another. Socially and vocationally they must have been a very cohesive group. There is a conciseness to the information, a lack of elaboration and explanation in each gospel that is answered to some degree in the synchronicity of all four. The gospel of John, written much later, is a supplemental gospel. He writes in consideration of the other writers. John, for instance, does not recount the baptism of Christ, as it is unnecessary for him to do so, but rather merely says that the Baptist bore record in 1:32-36. He writes in respect to the others, essential facts having been accounted for in other gospels, he lets the reader assume these things. He writes in awareness of Matthew, Mark and Luke, of whom he has a close relationship. He brings out facts that throw light on the earlier gospels, as we have seen regarding the disciple whom Jesus loved.

Now if we compare the story of the woman with the alabaster box of ointment who pours it upon Christ in all four gospels, Matthew 26, Mark 14, Luke 7:36, and John 11, we can see similarities and differences, and different pieces of information are presented to us. If we regard it as the same woman and the same event, one story described by four different sources, we can draw some conclusions. The facts presented in all gospels bring out a greater story.

Matthew and Mark show us that this story occurs in Bethany in the house of Simon the leper, while Luke shows us that it is a Pharisee's house, whose name was Simon; John writing later confides to us that it was in Bethany the house of Martha, Mary and Lazarus.

Although all gospels speak of the *woman*, the writers focus on different aspects of the story. Luke talks of

MARY MAGDALENE AND BETHANY

Christ's dealings with the Pharisee who had bidden Christ to eat with him, while Mark focuses on the woman, and her defence, and Matthew on the woman and the disciples' indignation, and the significance of what she had done. Luke speaks of her hospitality, while Mark speaks of the great work she has done in anointing his body before his burial. Mark and John both mention spikenard and the 300 pence. John gives us the name of Mary, the same one as paired with Martha, as the one who anointed the feet of Christ, and he focuses on the anointing, and he adds the fact that Judas was the son of Simon. He brings supplemental information to the story. John gives us a time, six days before the Passover, and the place, Bethany, where Lazarus was who had been dead, whom he had raised from the dead. He brings Lazarus into the account, as Luke has told us of the raising of Lazarus in his gospels. John shows Martha made and served him the supper, and that Mary took a pound of ointment of spikenard and anointed the feet of Jesus. Luke says that she stood at his feet behind him weeping, as their custom was to lay down on their front and sides to eat. He also records Jesus' words to Simon, the parable of the creditor with two debtors, and his fault in not making him welcome as the woman had done.

Although Luke introduces his gospel with the intent to "write unto you in order most excellent Theophilus," which he does at the beginning and the end, he does not everywhere write in a continuous chronology, as the others do. Luke has a potpourri of different stories in the middle of his narrative that have no regard to the chronology, and it is there we find the story of Jesus, the woman and Simon early in his gospel. This helps us to understand the difficulties in harmonizing all four accounts of the anointing of the woman. The story has regard to the last Passover as the other writers have placed it.

In Mark we have indignation amongst the disciples as to the waste of the ointment, that it could have been sold for 300 pence and given to the poor. He says that "Jesus said, Let her alone, she has done what she could, she is come aforehand to anoint my body for the burying." Also he reveals "Judas Iscariot went unto the chief priests to betray him." John tells us that the chief priests and the Pharisees had given a commandment, that if any man knew where he were, he should show it, that they might take him. Simon the leper was a Pharisee. Mark writes, chapter 11, "And when they heard it, they were glad, and promised to give him money. And he sought how he might conveniently betray him." John also talks of Judas Iscariot, defining him as "Simon's son, which should betray him," who asked, "Why was not this ointment sold for the poor?" and he adds that Judas had no concern for the poor, but had said it because he was a thief and had the bag. Jesus says, "Let her alone, against the day of my burying has she kept this." That the Mary who sits at Jesus' feet while her sister Martha, is cumbered with serving, is the same woman later who anoints him to the burial, makes perfect sense.

So we can conclude that all these differing accounts in the gospels are of the same story, that the house Jesus was in, the house of the Pharisee, Simon, was the house of Mary, Martha, and Lazarus in Bethany. *Martha* is

MARY MAGDALENE AND BETHANY

not a given name, but a title, it means "The Lady." She is the Lady of the house. Bethany was a village, yet also a suburb of Jerusalem. The Mary who had anointed Christ's feet was Mary Magdalene, the sinner, out of whom Christ had cast out seven devils. Martha's husband was Simon, known as the leper and a Pharisee. John, writing much later, is able to reveal other things, as he writes in a supplemental fashion—it is not by accident that he refers to a *Simon*, "Then said one of his disciples, Judas Iscariot, Simon's son, which should betray him," and given that this name appears in the context of the house of Bethany, that no other Simon was mentioned, the subtle inference is that this Simon must also be the father of the traitor, Judas Iscariot.

The gospel writers leave us to draw our conclusions, they do not tell us explicitly who is who. There is a tactfulness in the way events are described. Mark says they are in the house of Simon the leper in Bethany. He does not mention Martha or Mary. Luke calls it a Pharisee's house, and that his name is Simon. John pulls things together and tells us that it is in Bethany, where Lazarus was, with Martha and Mary, which Mary is the one who pours the ointment. Mark and Luke do not give us the name of the woman, but John says Mary. Luke tells us in chapter 10 that in a certain village lives Martha and Mary, where we have the story of Martha serving, and Mary taking the better part of hearing Christ's words. The gospels do not explicitly tell us certain things, they are left for us to work out. We can see then that Simon is Martha's husband, and the sister of Martha is Mary Magdalene, the weeping woman. Luke tells us she is the Mary called Magdalene, out of whom went seven devils. John also tells us that Judas is the son of Simon. John writes years after the other writers, when some things no longer need to be written with a regard for the sensibilities of folk living. That such a woman, who had sinned much, one whom Christ had exorcised of evil spirits, is allowed in the house of Simon, the Pharisee, knowing that she was a sinner, is explained by the fact that she is a relative, the sister of Martha, and she lives in the house. She is Mary, who once resided in Magdala, in Galilee, where she had lived a sinful life, but now lives with her sister Martha in Bethany. Magdala was a place on the western shore of the Lake of Galilee, about three miles south of Tiberias, one of Herod's cities. Over on the eastern shore, the land of the Gergesenes or Gadarenes we read of the man possessed of a legion of devils. Simon does not ask her to leave because she lives there, and has repented of her former life and listens to religious teaching. In Proverbs 7:10-12 young men are warned of the women of the night, "there met him a woman with the attire of an harlot, and subtle of heart. She is loud and stubborn; her feet abide not in her house: Now is she without, now in the streets, and lies in wait at every corner." Of such a display Mary would distance herself from, staying in the house, in order to also please the master of the house, Simon, the Pharisee, who would feel some embarrassment of having such a relative under his roof. We see this habit when Jesus would arrive for Lazarus, "Martha, as soon as she heard that Jesus was coming, went and met him: but Mary sat still in the house."

MARY MAGDALENE AND BETHANY

Now as we saw the name "Martha" means the Lady, it is not her name. As sister to Mary Magdalene, she would have come from Magdala in Galilee. She at some point married Simon. Her sister had been a source of shame to the family, having lived a loose life as a sinner. Mary, being of Magdala, was Mary Magdalene, who had repented and had come to be one of Christ's followers, as did Martha. Christ would visit them as he went through Bethany, and receive of Martha's hospitality, and Mary would sit at his feet learning of him. Simon would have welcomed his presence at first, depending on the nation's prevailing mood, but over time would follow the changing opinions of the Pharisee's councils, as they revolve in their minds the great question as to whether Jesus was the Messiah.

Let us consider the significance of this woman's act. Here she washes the feet of the one whose feet would soon crush the serpent in his death and resurrection, the one who was promised in the beginning, in Eden, immediately after the Fall. She wiped his *feet* with her hair and her tears. A woman, a *sinner*, as Luke says, kisses his feet. Here it is as if Eve herself were present in an act of contrition for her sins, the original sin of women. It is an amazing moment, unique and absolutely significant, a simply incredible act, that this woman performs. She would also, like an Eve, be at the empty tomb, upset at the disappearance of the body of Christ, who sees him as a gardener. Here then are references to the story of Genesis. It is not without a significant reason that of Mary Christ says, "Verily I say unto you, Wheresoever this gospel shall be preached throughout the whole world, this also that she has done shall be spoken of for a memorial of her."

She is Mary *Magdalene*. "Magdala" means "tower," this is the name by which Mary has come to be known. We find a *tower* in the Song of Solomon. We can compare this with the account of Mary and the resurrection in John, where various things happen. One can look at the Song of Songs chapters 4-5 and see it illustrated in this story of Mary Magdalene as written in the gospel of John. This Mary seems a living embodiment or fulfilment of the woman of the Song of Songs. Consider: she has "a neck like the tower of David, built for an armoury, whose breasts were like two young roes that feed among the lilies, until the day break, and the shadows flee away." Mary sits at Christ's feet learning of him, along with her sister, two young roes, feeding on his presence and his teaching. "I will get me to the mountain of myrrh and to the hill of frankincense," — Christ is anointed to death and burial. "There is no spot in you," or as Luke writes — "Wherefore I say unto you, her sins, which are many, are forgiven; for she loved much: but to whom little is forgiven, the same loves little. And he said unto her, Your sins are forgiven." She lingers around the garden where Christ is buried, until she meets him risen from the dead, as "the day has broken, the shadows are fled." — Luke 24:1, "Now upon the first day of the week, very early in the morning, they came to the sepulchre, bringing the spices which they had prepared, and certain others with them." And John 20:1, "The first day of the week comes Mary Magdalene early, when

MARY MAGDALENE AND BETHANY

it was yet dark, unto the sepulchre." Christ has been anointed with the perfumes to the burial, "She has done what she could: she is come aforehand to anoint my body to the burying," compare with, "the mountain of myrrh and frankincense." Mary meets one she thinks is the gardener. "Now in the place where he was crucified there was a garden; and in the garden a new sepulchre, wherein was never man yet laid." Compare with "He has come into *his garden*, gathered his myrrh with his spice," and "Now upon the first day of the week, very early in the morning, they came unto the sepulchre, bringing the spices which they had prepared." He has been anointed to the burying, the Song: "he has drunk his wine," Christ has spilled his blood, drunk the dregs of death. He bids us now to "eat O friends, drink abundantly O beloved." He offers us his body as food and his blood as wine. "He has put off his coat," the grave clothes are laid aside, "And he stooping down, and looking in, saw the linen clothes lying; . . . and the napkin, that was about his head, not lying with the linen clothes, but wrapped together in a place by itself." "he has washed his feet." Mary has washed his feet with her tears, "My beloved had withdrawn himself, and was gone, my soul failed when he spoke, I could not find him." "I know not where they have laid him," Mary tells the gardener, when "she knew not that it was Jesus." "The watchmen of the city smote me, wounded me."—Mary is treated with disdain by the Pharisee, she is not believed by the disciples. Luke writes, "It was Mary Magdalene, and Joanna, and Mary the mother of James, and other women that were with them, which told these things unto the apostles. And their words seemed to them as idle tales, and they believed them not." All these find the parallel in Mary's experience and the Song of Songs. Matthew and Mark recount Jesus' words, "Verily I say unto you, Wheresoever this gospel shall be preached throughout the whole world, this also that she has done shall be spoken of for a memorial of her."

Nothing of merit is said regarding Simon, however. He seems to be the very model of a Pharisee. He eyes the woman, his own relative, who is humbling herself before the Rabbi, with disgust. The Pharisee has desired him to eat at his house, yet he does not provide his guest with water to wash his feet, he does not greet him with a kiss, or anoint his head with oil. He has no regard for the repentance of Mary, or her adoration of the man of God. Not without reason he is not referred to directly in the gospels as Martha's husband, or as brother-in-law to Lazarus and Mary. It is as if he is not worthy to be remembered as one related to the friends of Christ—he, the one who condemns Mary the sinner as one to be avoided, is the real *leper*. John refuses to give him a memorial. It is Martha who serves Christ, and Mary who administers hospitality, not Simon. Simon questions Jesus' status as a prophet, one sent from God. As head of the house, he does not correct those who vilely questioned the use of the ointment upon his guest, that is Judas, his own son. It is likely he was one who questioned himself.

After the raising of Lazarus, "Then many of the Jews which came to Mary, and had seen the things which

MARY MAGDALENE AND BETHANY

Jesus did, believed on him. But some of them went their ways to the Pharisees, and told them what things Jesus had done." In John 11:57, the verse immediately before the account of Bethany, the Pharisees are recorded as having given commandment for information on Jesus' whereabouts, that he might be taken. Simon, being a Pharisee, would certainly have known of this warrant, in inviting Jesus to eat with him, perhaps he had told them what had happened with Lazarus. Here the one who shows no mercy to his relative, his prodigal sister-in-law, shows no mercy to Christ, but acts as one capable of bringing about Jesus' arrest, it could well be he was involved in telling Judas this information, and spurring him on to his crime. For as Mark writes of the events after the anointing with oil by Mary: "And Judas Iscariot, one of the twelve, went to the chief priests, to betray him unto them. And when they heard it, they were glad, and promised to give him money. And he sought how he might conveniently betray him." Simon was known as Simon the leper, whether as a nickname or in reality being one we do not know. If then a physical leper he is one who had consorted with Jesus but does not appear to have been healed by him. This implies that he had no real faith in Christ, as Jesus often asked for those seeking healing to believe. In his own country, Matthew 13:58, "he did not many mighty works there because of their unbelief." Hengstenberg writes, "By what figure could Pharisaism be better designated or described than by that of leprosy, by which man in a living body becomes an offensive and abhorred thing?"

The woman, Martha's sister, had a reputation as a

sinner. Simon was ashamed of her, she was the family secret. In Luke 7:39 "Simon spake within himself, saying, This man, if he were a prophet, would have known who and what manner of woman this is that touches him: for she is a sinner." Her very touch was regarded as filthy odium by Simon. His religion as a Pharisee was a religion of externals, it did not consist in a love for sinners. It did not admit of her being made known to the community, let alone having done an act that would be a memorial to the whole world. Simon would hide her in his house as if she were a leper, but Christ would make her a memorial to the whole world. He would keep her off the streets out of sight. In Luke, Jesus addressed this fault by telling Simon the story of two debtors, and his praise of her actions toward him. When asked by Jesus who would love the most his answer is a grudging, "I *suppose* the one forgiven the most." Here he shows Simon's sins, where he was at fault. With such a rebuke Simon could either respond with repentance for his sin, or hardheartedness and dislike toward Jesus. Simon's response was not recorded, but then this "I suppose" is telling, showing a reluctance to admit the truth. But John also reveals a clue, he says that Simon had a son. "Then said one of his disciples, Judas Iscariot, *Simon's son,* which should betray him, Why was not this ointment sold for three hundred pence, and given to the poor?" John reveals this astounding fact regarding Simon in the very passage of Mary anointing Christ for the burial. This is a subtle pointer to the identity of Simon. It was repeated at the Passover, "And supper being ended, the devil having

MARY MAGDALENE AND BETHANY

now put into the heart of Judas Iscariot, *Simon's son*, to betray him." He does not merely say that Judas Iscariot asked the question about the ointment being sold for the poor, but "Judas Iscariot, *son of Simon*." Now a person is regarded as the son of righteousness, in that righteousness is their father, or the son of wickedness, in that wickedness is their nature. We know Judas was a devil, John 6:70, "Jesus answered them, Have not I chosen you twelve, and one of you is a devil?" And the next verse, "He spake of Judas Iscariot *the son of Simon: for he it was that should betray him, being one of the twelve.*" John 13:26 repeats this association of the name of Judas with the name of Simon: "Jesus answered, He it is, to whom I shall give a sop, when I have dipped it. And when he had dipped the sop, he gave it to Judas Iscariot, *the son of Simon*." Here Judas is repeatedly described as the son of Simon, and this at the calling of the apostles, and also at the act of betrayal. As Simon is so is Judas. Judas is a devil and so also appears to be Simon. The implication of the repeated association of these two names is that the sin of Judas is also the sin of the father of Judas.

Judas is *given* the name *Iscariot*, Luke 22:3, "Then entered Satan into Judas surnamed Iscariot, being of the number of the twelve." *Iscariot* is not a surname in the sense that we take it. There is no trace Judas bore the name "Iscariot" before his betrayal. Hengstenberg says Iscariot means "the man of lies." John points out that he lied in feigning interest in giving the ointment money to the poor, as he had the bag, and was a thief. Iscariot then is a name given to distinguish him, post-betrayal, as Judas' family name is actually *son of Simon*. "He gave it to Judas Iscariot, the son of Simon." He is the man of lies, as much as he is the son of perdition, the man of sin. Similarly Peter is Simon son of Jona, and James and John sons of Zebedee. This is how paternity is expressed in the New Testament world. "Surnamed" means to put a name upon, it does not necessarily mean a surname as we have and receive from our father. It comes from *kaleho*, meaning to give a name to, call his name, to be called, that is, to bear a name among men. It is a given name. Judas then is the man of lies, Simon's son.

Matthew says regarding the use of the precious ointment, "when his disciples saw it, they had indignation," and Mark says, "there were some who had indignation within themselves," while Luke makes no mention of the disciples' indignation, but talks rather of the revulsion of the Pharisee upon seeing the woman who used the ointment touch the Rabbi, but John points to the source of the indignation, "Then said one of his disciples, Judas Iscariot, Simon's son, which should betray him, Why was not this ointment sold for three hundred pence, and given to the poor?" The source of the complaint then was Judas and by association, and what we have read of Simon in Luke, Simon himself. Judas took the cue from his father on the matter. Judas and Simon were like peas in a pod. When addressing Simon with the parable of the two debtors, Christ relates of one who owed and was forgiven 500 pence, a figure greater than the 300 of the ointment that they were complaining about. Here Christ is addressing

MARY MAGDALENE AND BETHANY

the idea of parsimony with money, it is not to be quibbled about, particularly as it regards a burial, and the burial of the very Son of God at that. John writes that, "Jesus said, Let her alone, she has done what she could, she is come aforehand to anoint my body for the burying." Here Judas and the others involved, are, in effect, quibbling about the cost of Christ's burial preparations, and the Lord gives these dolts an angry, harsh rebuke. Christ had said of the Pharisees, "they swallow a camel and strain at a gnat," in other words, they are reluctant to let go of anything they have swallowed from out their bowels to the draught, they are constipated in covetousness. They would not give anything of themselves, not even a scat. They are the antithesis of generosity. Simon gives no water, no kiss, no oil. His thoughts give no trust, no faith, toward the Rabbi Jesus, "if this man were a prophet—" They give no forgiveness, no mercy, no charity, to the woman, his sister, his flesh and blood,— "he would know *this woman* is a *sinner*." Every thought drips with contempt. Such a father would beget a Judas.

So here we have a family scene, another hidden story, the identity of the weeping woman comes into view, and also a disgraceful episode, that of the husband of Martha and his son. There is a warmth and beauty regarding the love and hospitality of Martha, Mary and Lazarus, among whom a death unfolds a resurrection in Lazarus. Yet, like all families there is a sad and dark side, where here an evil paternity plays out a wicked story, even the betrayal of Christ, with the hopeless suicide of Judas, and this story is delicately implied

THERE CAME ONE RUNNING

in the gospel narrative. Yet the main import from this story, which eclipses the darker elements of Simon and Judas, is the love of this house in Martha, Mary and Lazarus, and the identity of Mary Magdalene. In her we have a magnificent story of womanhood, as Christ said, one who would, in all the world, be lauded in a memorial of what she had done, in her love toward Christ and her act in anointing him to the burial and witnessing the resurrection.

It is a story like that of Mark's, one that is not given prominence, so as not to hinder the intent of the gospel writers to present to us the glory of Christ himself, but nevertheless it is written between the lines, and when understood, shows us more of the glory of the one who orchestrates all things to his own will.

18. The Lord's Brothers
~

Is not this the carpenter's son? is not his mother called
Mary? and his brothers, James, and Joses, and Simon, and
Judas? — *Matthew 13:55*

And he ordained twelve, that they should be with him,
and that he might send them forth to preach, And to have
power to heal sicknesses, and to cast out devils: And
Simon he surnamed Peter; And James the son of Zebedee,
and John the brother of James; and he surnamed them
Boanerges, which is, The sons of thunder: And Andrew,
and Philip, and Bartholomew, and Matthew, and Thomas,
and James the son of Alphaeus, and Thaddaeus, and
Simon the Canaanite, And Judas Iscariot, which also
betrayed him: and they went into an house.

—*Mark 3:14*

There came then his brothers and his mother, and, standing
without, sent unto him, calling him. And the multitude sat
about him, and they said unto him, "Behold, your mother
and your brothers without seek for you. "And he answered
them, saying, "Who is my mother, or my brothers?" And
he looked round about on them which sat about him, and
said, "Behold my mother and my brothers! For whosoever
shall do the will of God, the same is my brother, and my
sister, and mother."

—*Mark 3:31-35*

WHO IS MY mother and my brothers? Jesus asks in the third chapter of Mark. Here we shall examine this question. The gospel writers wrote to ascribe importance to their main subject, the person and acts of Christ, while leaving certain subsidiary details as to the identity of various people, including the members of Jesus' family, as briefly noted or merely implied, even by a single reference. These answers can bring out hidden stories in the narrative. We will see how the answer to this can give light on the first three chapters of Mark in the next chapter, where the events of chapter three form a distinct climax, if we understand the relations in his family.

Firstly, the Virgin Mary, the mother of Jesus, had a sister, who it appears was also called *Mary*. She was the wife of Cleophas, as John 19:25 reveals:

> Now there stood by the cross of Jesus his mother, and his mother's sister, Mary the wife of Cleophas, and Mary Magdalene.

Mark 15:40 shows us that this Mary was the mother of James the Less, Joses and Salome:

> There were also women looking on afar off: among whom was Mary Magdalene, and Mary the mother of James the less and of Joses, and Salome.

And in Matthew 10:3, we see that this James is also the son of Alphaeus:

> Philip, and Bartholomew; Thomas, and Matthew the publican; James the son of Alphaeus, and Lebbaeus, whose surname was Thaddaeus;

Joses and Salome then would also be children of Alphaeus. Now *Cleophas* is the Aramaic equivalent of the Hebrew *Alphaeus*. Both mean "changing." They are the same person. The apostle James is known as the Lord's brother in Galatians 1:19: "But other of the

THE LORD'S BROTHERS

apostles saw I none, save James the Lord's brother." It follows then that also Joses and Salome are brother and sister to the Lord. In Mark 6:3 the Nazarenes in the synagogue ask the question, "Is not this the carpenter, the son of Mary, the brother of James, and Joses, and of Juda, and Simon? and are not his sisters here with us?" So also Juda and Simon are brothers to the Lord. Now the brothers of Jesus are in fact his *cousins*, not *direct* brothers. Cousins in the middle eastern world were also referred to as *brothers*. Mark 12:19 gives us an insight:

> Master, Moses wrote unto us, "If a man's brother die, and leave his wife behind him, and leave no children, that his brother should take his wife, and raise up seed unto his brother."

We see that familial relations can work in this way, that brothers extend across uncles or aunts, not that this was the case here, but we see the tendency.

James' brother is Judas or Jude, as shown in the letter of Jude:

> Jude, the servant of Jesus Christ, and brother of James, to them that are sanctified by God the Father, and preserved in Jesus Christ, and called:

In Matthew 10:2-3 Jude is also called Lebbaeus, meaning a man of heart, and whose surname was Thaddaeus, which means large hearted and courageous:

> Now the names of the twelve apostles are these; The first, Simon, who is called Peter, and Andrew his brother; James the son of Zebedee, and John his brother; Philip, and Bartholomew; Thomas, and Matthew the publican; James the son of Alphaeus, and *Lebbaeus*, whose surname was Thaddaeus;

Now in Luke 6:14-16 the *apostles* include James the son of Alphaeus, and Simon called Zelotes and Judas the brother of James.

> Simon, (whom he also named Peter,) and Andrew his brother, James and John, Philip and Bartholomew, Matthew and Thomas, James the son of Alphaeus, and Simon called Zelotes, And Judas the brother of James, and Judas Iscariot, which also was the traitor.

We read Mark 6:3 that Jesus' brothers are "James and Joses and Simon and Jude." The apostles are listed in the same order, "James the son of Alphaeus, and Simon called Zelotes, and Judas (Lebbaeus) the brother of James."

> Mark 6: James and Joses and Simon and Jude.

> Luke 6: James the son of Alphaeus, and Simon called Zelotes, and Judas the brother of James.

This arrangement would suggest that this Simon the Zealot, or Zelotes is also in fact one of Jesus' brothers. Matthew 10:4 calls him "Simon the Canaanite," which means *zealous*.

Of course in Mark's list we see that another brother of Jesus is *Joses*, as also in Matthew 13:55:

> Is not this the carpenter's son? is not his mother called Mary? and his brothers, James, and *Joses*, and Simon, and Judas?

Joses was by the apostles known as *Barnabas*. He was a Levite of Cyprus. We read in Acts 4:36:

> And Joses, who by the apostles was surnamed Barnabas, (which is, being interpreted, The son of consolation,) a

Levite, and of the country of Cyprus,

Perhaps this accounted for him being absent among the gospel accounts, yet present in the Acts, as he played a central role in the first missionary journey with Paul and Mark to Cyprus. If Joses is a Levite then Alphaeus, or Cleophas, Mary's husband, was a Levite.

Mark 6:3 adds, "and are not his sisters here with us?" Mark 15:40-41 says, "There were also women looking on afar off: among whom was Mary Magdalene, and Mary the mother of James the less and of Joses, and Salome. (Who also, when he was in Galilee, followed him, and ministered unto him;) and many other women which came up with him unto Jerusalem." And Mark 16:1 says, "And when the sabbath was past, Mary Magdalene, and Mary the mother of James, and Salome, had bought sweet spices, that they might come and anoint him." So Jesus has sisters as well, one is called Salome, whose mother is Mary, who together bring spices to anoint the body of her esteemed cousin. Salome was a follower of Jesus, and ministered to him.

Now, as we have suggested, the name order of the apostles and brothers implies that Simon the Zealot is a brother, similarly we have two passages regarding the women, if we compare Mark 15:40 with Matthew 27:56. Both are referring to the time just after Jesus died:

> There were also women looking on afar off: among whom was Mary Magdalene, and Mary the mother of James the less and of Joses, and Salome;

> Among which was Mary Magdalene, and Mary the mother of James and Joses, and the mother of Zebedee's children.

The name order is the same—Mary Magdalene, Mary the mother of James and Joses; and while Mark names Salome, Matthew puts it, "the mother of Zebedee's children." This would suggest that Zebedee was married to Salome, the sister of Jesus, and that she was mother to James and John. And this would explain the confidence with which, "then came to him the mother of Zebedee's children with her sons, worshipping him, and desiring a certain thing of him... Grant that these my two sons may sit, the one on your right hand, and the other on the left, in your kingdom." It is the confidence of a sister to ask such a request. Jesus had called James and John, who were partners with Simon Peter and Andrew thus in Mark 1:19-20:

> And when he had gone a little further thence, he saw James the son of Zebedee, and John his brother, who also were in the ship mending their nets. And straightway he called them: and they left their father Zebedee in the ship with the hired servants, and went after him.

That the mother of James and John requested these favours ties in with the fact that Salome was his follower and ministered to him, while her husband continued the family fishing business with the hired help. James and John, then, were related to Jesus, as *nephews*.

Now in Colossians 4:10 Paul writes,

> Aristarchus my fellowprisoner salutes you, and Marcus, sister's son to Barnabas, (touching whom you received commandments: if he come to you, receive him;)

Here we see again, as we have examined at length in this book, that Mark or Marcus, is related to the family of Christ, in that he is Barnabas's sister's son. He is

THE LORD'S BROTHERS

one from whom they have "received commandments," commandment here is in Greek an *entolé*. It has its root in the word *telos*, the end to which all things relate, the aim, purpose. Paul says to the Athenians,

> And the times of this ignorance God winked at; but now *commands* all men every where to repent: Because he has appointed a day, in the which he will judge the world in righteousness by that man whom he has ordained; whereof he has given assurance unto all men, in that he has raised him from the dead.

Here the command is *the gospel,* and here it is connected to the last day, the day of judgement, so we have an end to which all things relate. Thus we can regard this word *commandments* simply as a pointer to Mark's gospel where in verse 14-15 of the first chapter we have, "Jesus came into Galilee, preaching the gospel of the kingdom of God, and saying, The time is fulfilled, and the kingdom of God is at hand: repent ye, and believe the gospel." No wonder Paul charges the Colossians to receive such a one if he come unto them.

Given these relations between Alphaeus, or Cleophas, Joses or Barnabas the Levite, and Mark or Marcus, and the link with Cyprus, one might surmise this part of the family were in business, trading between Cyprus and Palestine, and, given what we have concluded about Mark, who was of a wealthy family, perhaps it was in the linen trade.

Barnabas was known as "a Levite," as if it were a nickname, given to Cypriots as if he were a familiar personality, as of one who would often visit as a trader. He came in late to the story, in Acts 4:36, "being a Levite, and of the country of Cyprus, having land, sold it, and brought the money, and laid it at the apostles' feet." We know Barnabas was "the son of consolation," one who had a fond position with his father, when another son had once proved a disappointment to a father's expectations, such a one who was involved in the family business would fit. The family comes from the Galilee where both the use of boats and the growth of flax crops suggest a possibility of ocean trade and linen goods. Barnabas seems to have held a permanent position on Cyprus, he knew many people there, as he took Paul on the missionary journey with Mark, perhaps he was the business representative there for his father, and he seemed to be familiar with Antioch. Earlier in Mark 2:21-22, Jesus had made a reference to new cloth on old clothes, and patches on old wineskins, so in Galilee there would most certainly have been a trade of wine, vineyards and linen.

Perhaps Joses reflected the older son of the Prodigal story, who as the father of the two says, in verses 31-32, "Son, you are ever with me, and all that I have is yours. It was meet that we should make merry, and be glad: for this your brother was dead, and is alive again; and was lost, and is found." For some reason Barnabas was absent from the gospel story but he now comes with great generosity, having sold land, giving it to the church, it seems the penitent action of someone, a wealthy person, who has come to a greater understanding. Christ's references always were grounded in the lives of the people about him. These are but suppositions, but inferences can be made between all these lines.

Now in the last chapter of Luke we find the account

THE LORD'S BROTHERS

of the resurrection of Christ, and his appearance to his disciples. He had been buried the day before the sabbath, and Mary Magdalene, Joanna, and Mary the mother of James, and other women returned on the first day of the week to the sepulchre bringing spices. To their surprise there was no body, but two men in shining garments standing by said "why seek ye the living among the dead? He is not here, but is risen: remember how he spake unto you when he was yet in Galilee, saying, The Son of man must be delivered into the hands of sinful men, and be crucified, and the third day rise again?" They told all these things unto the eleven, and to all the rest, who did not believe them, Peter ran unto the sepulchre to see, and departed, wondering at what had come to pass. Now two of them were travelling to Emmaus, about threescore furlongs, they were met by the risen Christ, hidden to their eyes, in which they had a conversation which continued into a house where they broke bread, upon which their eyes were opened, they realised who he was, and Jesus disappeared. They rose up and went to Jerusalem to the eleven gathered there and told them what had happened, and how he was known to them in the breaking of bread. As they thus spake Jesus himself stood in the midst of them, and said, "Peace be unto you!" They thought he was a spirit, then he said, "Why are ye troubled? and why do thoughts arise in your hearts? Behold my hands and my feet, that it is I myself: handle me, and see; for a spirit has not flesh and bones, as ye see me have." They believed, and then he ate some fish and an honey comb, and said, "These are the words which I spake unto you, while I was yet with you, that all things must be fulfilled, which were written in the law of Moses, and in the prophets, and in the Psalms, concerning me."And then he said unto them, "Thus it is written, and thus it behoved Christ to suffer, and to rise from the dead the third day: And that repentance and remission of sins should be preached in his name among all nations, beginning at Jerusalem. And ye are witnesses of these things. And, behold, I send the promise of my Father upon you: but tarry ye in the city of Jerusalem, until ye be endued with power from on high."

Now one of the two disciples on the road to Emmaus is named, and he was *Cleopas*, who as we have seen is *Alphaeus*, husband of Mary, the Virgin's sister, father of the cousins or brothers of Jesus, in other words, Jesus' uncle. They were travelling away from the city and the other disciples on a significant day, that of the resurrection, and here Jesus reins them in, as they would abruptly return to the City. Jesus had approached them and said, "What manner of communications are these that ye have one to another, as you walk, and are sad?" They are sad because of his death, and have not expected, as he had promised that he would indeed rise on the third day. One would assume they are travelling north to attend to pressing business matters. Jesus is making a significant appearance to his uncle with his companion, somewhat like to Saul, on the road to Damascus. One can only guess who the companion might have been, probably a partner, perhaps it was Joses, as we know the eleven are in Jerusalem. So here Cleopas, the father of his brothers receives a special appearance, and

THE LORD'S BROTHERS

this would seem natural to Jesus as the law specified honour to fathers, and uncles, as it were, here a significant member of Christ's family, the husband of Mary his mother's sister, the mother of his brothers/cousins. So we are seeing in these appearances, his disciples, his brothers and his mother, and his aunt and uncle with his sisters. Barnabas' role in the first missionary journey suggests that he would have seen the risen Lord, and perhaps it was on the road to Emmaus.

Another thing is significant, and that is the reference to the breaking of bread. Verses 30-31 says, "And it came to pass, as he sat at meat with them, he took bread, and blessed it, and brake, and gave to them, and their eyes were opened, and they knew him; and he vanished out of their sight." When they had returned to the eleven, in reporting how he was known to them in the breaking of bread, even as they spake, "Jesus himself stood in the midst of them, and said to them, Peace be unto you." The breaking of bread was the common point in which Christ was to make himself known, as it is was in the early church and continues with us today in the Eucharist. In doing this he shows the significance of the Lord's Supper, that it is in this way and by these means that he is to be known.

Jesus as the shepherd of the sheep, reins these two breakaways back into the fold, and then reveals himself to all, who are now gathered together. Here he shows us his flesh and his bones, and that he also eats, that his body has risen from the grave in perfect order, in a meal of fish and honeycomb. Here his body is made whole, and also the greater body of his family are gathered together, all partaking of that same bread.

Matthew is called

Now Levi, or Matthew the publican, or tax collector, is also "the son of Alphaeus." Here in Mark 2:14 his name suggests he is a Levite.

> And as he passed by, he saw Levi the son of Alphaeus sitting at the receipt of custom, and said unto him, "Follow me." And he arose and followed him.

Matthew then is one of the brothers or cousins of Jesus. As we saw earlier the name order of the apostles would suggest that Simon is a brother of Christ. We could also apply this same device to that of Matthew, as the names are recounted thus in Matthew's account:

> Philip, and Bartholomew; Thomas, and Matthew the publican; James the son of Alphaeus, and Lebbaeus, whose surname was Thaddaeus (Jude).

The name of *Matthew* directly precedes that of James the less, the brother of the Lord. In Mark 3:18 and Luke 6:15, however, the order is different, they put *Thomas* after Matthew and before James, but Matthew makes the point of putting his name immediately before James the son of Alphaeus. These subtle changes are telling. He places himself with his brothers.

Matthew and Luke recount the genealogies of the Lord's family. Jesus' genealogy echoes with these names. In Luke 3:24 *Levi* the son of Melchi is the son of *Matthat* and also the son of *Joseph*, who would be Matthew's uncle, the husband of the Virgin Mary, of whom was born Jesus.

THE LORD'S BROTHERS

> Which was the son of Matthat, which was the son of Levi, which was the son of Melchi, which was the son of Janna, which was the son of Joseph,

Here we see the age old custom of naming children after their ancestors. Matthat and Levi hang together, as much as Levi is Matthew. Perhaps he became Matthew when he followed Jesus, as it means "gift of God," in that he is restored back to his father and family, as we shall see shortly. *Simeon* also is an ancestor and Simon is one of the brothers. Another ancestor in verse 29 is *Joses*, also one of Jesus' brothers.

> Which was the son of Jose, which was the son of Eliezer, which was the son of Jorim, which was the son of Matthat, which was the son of Levi,

Joses, being Barnabas, with his links in Cyprus, would perhaps be absent from the epochal events in Judea, unless he was that one with Cleopas on the way to Emmaus.

Now Matthew is also absent from this list of Jesus' brothers. This absence could be explained on another reason, that of *notoriety,* and it could also be on the basis of all the gospel writers' tendency to self deprecation. Now if we assume Matthew is one of the brothers then we need to account as to why Matthew was not mentioned here in Nazareth as one of the brothers, when Jesus had preached in the synagogue. Jesus came from Nazareth, where because of familiarity, "they could do no miracles there because of their unbelief," but Matthew was in Capernaum, where his job was tax collecting for the Romans, otherwise known as a *publican*. It was Matthew, in chapter 18:15-17, who wrote these words of Jesus,

> Moreover if your brother shall trespass against you, go and tell him his fault between you and him alone: if he shall hear you, you have gained your brother. But if he will not hear you, then take with you one or two more, that in the mouth of two or three witnesses every word may be established. And if he shall neglect to hear them, tell it unto the church: but if he neglect to hear the church, let him be unto you as an heathen man and a publican.

Collecting taxes for the Romans was seen as a traitorous, odious activity, such as would make one a heathen man and a publican. Matthew was the black sheep of the family, escaping to another town, to Capernaum. Now Joses or Barnabas was called "the son of consolation," the scripture makes a point of noting this, perhaps it was because Joses proved a joy to his father Alphaeus, in the place of a son who had proved a disappointment, for a time at least, to his father. Similarly when Cain proved a disappointment to Adam and Eve, Seth was conceived, and his name means, like consolation, "compensation." Joses being a Levite of Cyprus, must have had an intimacy with his father, travelling abroad with him. His brother, however had gone to the Romans as a tax collector, and so was regarded as a heathen man and a publican, a disappointment, while Joses proved to be the consolation. Jesus was to seek out the prodigal and bring him back to his father, if we understand it in this fashion. The words just quoted from Matthew, Jesus' words as it happens, speak of dissension and reconciliation between brothers—"if he shall hear you, you have gained your brother." Matthew certainly

THE LORD'S BROTHERS

hears his brothers words, as he is to write them, and this teaching is only in Matthew.

In the calling of Matthew Jesus brings "two or three witnesses"—the crowd in the house with the healing of the paralytic, the preaching of Jesus by the seaside, and Jesus himself calling him. That heathen man and publican that was Levi was left behind at the seat of custom, as Matthew joined his brother to go to the feast. It is Matthew who recorded these words in 21:28-32:

> "But what think you? A certain man had two sons; and he came to the first, and said, Son, go work to day in my vineyard. He answered and said, I will not: but afterward he repented, and went. And he came to the second, and said likewise. And he answered and said, I go, sir: and went not. Which of the two did the will of his father?" They say to him, "The first." Jesus said to them, "Truly I say to you, That the publicans and the harlots go into the kingdom of God before you. For John came unto you in the way of righteousness, and you believed him not: but the publicans and the harlots believed him: and you, when you had seen it, repented not afterward, that you might believe him."

Here Jesus speaks of a certain man, *certain* being as one who was known to the disciples, who has two sons, one went to work for him, the other did not. The son is told to work in the vineyard, but said, "I will not," but afterward changed his mind and went. Jesus then adds "the publicans and harlots go into the kingdom of God." Here we have Matthew, who in real life, refuses his father's, or the family business to follow a more lucrative tax collecting. The second son says, "I go sir," and went not. Joses is away from the events in Judea, attending Alphaeus' business, but he does not go to the work in the Lord's vineyard, as his other brothers, until later of course, when he takes Paul and Mark to Cyprus. These family dynamics spin around these parables in interesting ways. It seems natural that Jesus might take the events in his own life and family circle and weave them into his parables. Again, "if he shall hear you you have gained your brother," —it is Matthew who is relating these stories, and he has heard his brother/cousin Jesus. The pharisees did not believe John the Baptist, but the publicans and harlots did, and repented *afterward*. Matthew indeed "goes into the kingdom of God," and takes his place as one of the judges of the twelve tribes of Israel, as an apostle and an evangelist, a writer of a gospel, as one who does the will of his Father, one who has heard and sought after Christ. "Behold, your mother and your brothers without seek for you." Jesus would ask, "Who is my mother or my brothers?" and he answers, "Behold my mother and my brothers! For whosoever shall do the will of God, the same is my brother, and my sister, and mother." One who had served the Romans now pens a gospel filled with Old Testament prophecies, a gospel aimed in the first instance to Hebrews, while Mark's is aimed more at a Latin audience.

When Jesus had preached in Nazareth he could do no healings because of their unbelief. Now in Capernaum there was no such unbelief as Matthew's calling was in relation to the healing of the man sick of the palsy, as we see in the account of Matthew's calling in Mark 2:1-17,

And again he entered into Capernaum after some days; and it was noised that he was in the house. And straightway many were gathered together, insomuch that there was no room to receive them, no, not so much as about the door:

THE LORD'S BROTHERS

and he preached the word unto them. And they come unto him, bringing one sick of the palsy, which was borne of four. And when they could not come nigh unto him for the press, they uncovered the roof where he was: and when they had broken it up, they let down the bed wherein the sick of the palsy lay. When Jesus saw their faith, he said unto the sick of the palsy, "Son, your sins be forgiven you." But there were certain of the scribes sitting there, and reasoning in their hearts, "Why doth this man thus speak blasphemies? Who can forgive sins but God only?" And immediately when Jesus perceived in his spirit that they so reasoned within themselves, he said unto them, "Why reason ye these things in your hearts? Whether is it easier to say to the sick of the palsy, Your sins be forgiven you; or to say, Arise, and take up your bed, and walk? But that ye may know that the Son of man has power on earth to forgive sins," (he said to the sick of the palsy,) "I say unto you, Arise, and take up your bed, and go your way into thine house." And immediately he arose, took up the bed, and went forth before them all; insomuch that they were all amazed, and glorified God, saying, "We never saw it on this fashion." And he went forth again by the sea side; and all the multitude resorted unto him, and he taught them. And as he passed by, he saw Levi the son of Alphaeus sitting at the receipt of custom, and said unto him, "Follow me." And he arose and followed him. And it came to pass, that, as Jesus sat at meat in his house, many publicans and sinners sat also together with Jesus and his disciples: for there were many, and they followed him. And when the scribes and Pharisees saw him eat with publicans and sinners, they said unto his disciples, "How is it that he eats and drinks with publicans and sinners?" When Jesus heard it, he said unto them, "They that are whole have no need of the physician, but they that are sick: I came not to call the righteous, but sinners to repentance."

The healing of the sick man was to show that Christ, the son of man, had power to forgive sins, even heathens and publicans. One must picture the scene—Matthew, sitting in view of the house nearby at the receipt of custom. He observed Christ entering in the house, the crowd filing in, the four men bearing the paralytic on his bed attempt to go in, failing this they ascend to remove the roof and lower the man in. Then presently the tax collector, idle at his seat of custom, as the customers have gathered around the house, sees the man walking out carrying his bed, and walking past him. He then observes Jesus then coming out, approaching the seaside, where a crowd forms around him, to whom he preaches. Matthew hears the message over at his desk, and then Christ passes by Matthew and says to him, "Follow me." They then go to a feast where many publicans and sinners attended. One can imagine perhaps Mary Magdalene may have been present. Mark 16:9 tells us she had been delivered of seven devils, and it was only recently in Mark 1:34 that Jesus had cast out many devils.

Similarly in Luke 15 many publicans and sinners came to eat with Christ, and there he speaks of the prodigal son and also the shepherd leaving the ninety nine to seek out the lost sheep, perhaps this is what Matthew hears from the seaside sermon. "And when he has found it, he lays it on his shoulders, rejoicing. And when he comes home, he calls together his friends and neighbours, saying unto them, Rejoice with me; for I have found my sheep which was lost." Jesus goes after his lost brother and finds him, and here Jesus goes to rejoice with Matthew and his friends at a feast, he rejoices with the sheep he had lost. In Matthew 11:19 we read, "The Son of man came eating and drinking, and they say, Behold a man gluttonous, and a winebibber,

THE LORD'S BROTHERS

a friend of publicans and sinners." This is where the sheep have gone astray, here he is the shepherd and bishop of souls. He had spoken of the parable of the woman who had lost the coin, here Matthew is at the receipt of custom counting his money. The account of the prodigal son is preceded by the parable of the woman who having ten silver coins, loses one, lights a lamp, sweeps the house and searches carefully until she finds it. Now Jesus gathers twelve apostles, but he seeks one out in Matthew, who is the last to be called. In Matthew 4:16-18 we read: "The people which sat in darkness saw great light; and to them which sat in the region and shadow of death light is sprung up. From that time Jesus began to preach, and to say, Repent: for the kingdom of heaven is at hand," then he adds in verses 18-19, "and Jesus, walking by the sea of Galilee, saw two brothers, Simon called Peter, and Andrew his brother, casting a net into the sea: for they were fishers. And he says unto them, Follow me, and I will make you fishers of men." Here Christ is the lamp, he sweeps the house for the lost coin, he begins to preach, and searches carefully until he finds it, walking by the sea he first calls Peter and Andrew, then in 2:14, we have, "And *finally* as he passed by, he saw Levi the son of Alphaeus sitting at the receipt of custom, and said unto him, Follow me. And he arose and followed him." It is as if the woman finds the lost coin.

Then with the parable of the prodigal son, Christ concludes, in verse 32, "It was meet that we should make merry, and be glad: for this your brother was dead, and is alive again; and was lost, and is found."

THERE CAME ONE RUNNING

It was like Jeremiah's word, chapter 50:6, "My people has been lost sheep: their shepherds have caused them to go astray, they have turned them away on the mountains: they have gone from mountain to hill, they have forgotten their resting place." Matthew has gone astray and forgotten his resting place. Jesus goes after his lost brother and finds him, not only that, but like the father with the prodigal, who puts his best robe on him, a ring on his hand, and shoes on his feet, he ordains him an apostle and an evangelist. It seems that Jesus' parables and stories would have a basis in actual happenings and relationships, in the things he was doing, all things happened around him, all things worked together in an amazing flood of providence. If our assumption that Matthew is a brother is right, Jesus is calling and convincing his errant cousin, forgiving him for his straying, by means of a miraculous healing. The sick man was a paralytic, unable to walk, and here Matthew, sitting at the receipt of custom, the toll house, bound to his seat, is called to follow, to walk after Christ.

Not long after, up on the mountain, Jesus calls him to be one of the twelve, as Mark 3:14 shows:

> And he ordained twelve, that they should be with him, and that he might send them forth to preach, And to have power to heal sicknesses, and to cast out devils: And Simon he surnamed Peter; and James the son of Zebedee, and John the brother of James; and he surnamed them Boanerges, which is, The sons of thunder: And Andrew, and Philip, and Bartholomew, and Matthew, and Thomas, and James the son of Alphaeus, and Thaddaeus, and Simon the Canaanite, And Judas Iscariot, which also betrayed him: and they went into an house.

THE LORD'S BROTHERS

Immediately they remove down from the mountain "into an house," that is to an inhabited area, among the multitude. Having established these facts we can look at the first three chapters of Mark and see the glory of Christ in a fresh and clear light.

19. Jesus Masters The Multitude

By the way of the sea, beyond Jordan, in Galilee of the nations. the people that walked in darkness have seen a great light: they that dwell in the land of the shadow of death, upon them has the light shined. You have multiplied the nation, and not increased the joy: they joy before you according to the joy in harvest, and as men rejoice when they divide the spoil. For you have broken the yoke of his burden, and the staff of his shoulder, the rod of his oppressor, as in the day of Midian. For every battle of the warrior is with confused noise, and garments rolled in blood; but this shall be with burning and fuel of fire. For unto us a child is born, unto us a son is given: and the government shall be upon his shoulder: and his name shall be called Wonderful, Counsellor, The mighty God, The everlasting Father, The Prince of Peace. Of the increase of his government and peace there shall be no end, upon the throne of David, and upon his kingdom, to order it, and to establish it with judgment and with justice from henceforth even for ever. The zeal of the LORD of hosts will perform this.
—*Isaiah 9:1-7*

MARK'S GOSPEL BURSTS upon us in many immediatelys and straightways, as Jesus the Christ comes in from the wilderness to preach the gospel. We will pick up various salient points in a survey of these events. Here we see the fulfilment of our text in that word of Isaiah the prophet regarding the way of the sea beyond Jordan in Galilee of the nations.

In the beginning of the gospel of Mark, we read that

JESUS MASTERS THE MULTITUDE

at the coming of John the Baptist "all the land of Judea was baptised in the Jordan." Then in 1:21-22 Jesus is said to have preached "as one having authority and not as the scribes, he commands even the unclean spirits, who cry, 'Let us alone!' " Christ is cleansing the land of spiritual wickedness. He is casting out the devil. In verse 29 they enter the house of Simon and Andrew in Capernaum, and Jesus heals Simon's wife's mother who is sick. While praying in a solitary place his disciples find him and tell him "all men seek for you." They then go into the next towns, he goes into the synagogues and casts out devils. In verse 45 the "multitude come to him from every quarter." Chapter 2:2 reads, "in Capernaum many were gathered together," in verse 13, "all the multitude resorted to him," Jesus is in a house, where the paralytic is let down in through the roof because of the press of the crowd, and he forgives and heals him. Then we have the call of Matthew. In chapter 3:2 Jesus heals a man with a withered hand on the Sabbath, it was then that the Pharisees took counsel with the Herodians against him. In verse seven "a great multitude followed him, and from Judea, Jerusalem, Idumaea, from beyond Jordan, Tyre and Sidon came to him," and he healed many, and unclean spirits fell down before him. And finally in chapter 3:13, upon a mountain, he ordained twelve that they should be with him to preach, heal the sick and cast out devils.

In chapter 4:23-25 Matthew sums up what Mark relates in these first chapters:

> And Jesus went about all Galilee, teaching in their synagogues, and preaching the gospel of the kingdom, and

healing all manner of sickness and all manner of disease among the people. And his fame went throughout all Syria: and they brought unto him all sick people that were taken with divers diseases and torments, and those which were possessed with devils, and those which were lunatic, and those that had the palsy; and he healed them. And there followed him great multitudes of people from Galilee, and from Decapolis, and from Jerusalem, and from Judaea, and from beyond Jordan.

The *multitudes* are a key part in the development of the events in the gospel story. They are a personality in themselves. The *crowd* is sick, troubled by the demon possessed, swayed by the wicked, curious and needy, hungry and thirsty, dangerous at times, all seeking Christ. So in chapter 6:1 it proved a necessity for Jesus to feed these people, many had run there on foot from all the cities, his disciples suggested they go to the villages, but they must have already proved a drain on resources, and similarly in chapter 8 they had not eaten for three days, so it was that in his compassion Jesus would feed them miraculously. This emerged from the necessity of this great multitude come to see him from all quarters.

We get the impression of a growing press of humanity. In chapter 1:33 the whole city is gathered at the door, after the healing of the leper, who was commanded to keep quiet, yet proclaimed it freely, in that Jesus was unable to openly enter that city, but was outside in deserted places, and then they came to him there from every direction. A few days later, in 2:1, he enters Capernaum, and immediately many gather together so there was no longer room to receive people, not even near the door. It grows to the point in 3:7-8, where a great multitude from Judea and Jerusalem and Idumaea

JESUS MASTERS THE MULTITUDE

and beyond the Jordan and those from Tyre and Sidon heard how many things he was doing and came to him, and he had to tell his disciples to ready a small boat lest they should crush him. From such boats he could preach, and also cross over to get away to deal with other matters.

Here we have the background to the events that were soon to follow in chapter three. We have the common themes—Jesus preaches with authority and not as the scribes, the growth of a great multitude pressed upon him and his followers from every quarter, the houses he enters are beset by crowds, he casts out devils and heals people. The authorities are forming an opposition to him because he has transgressed their Sabbath. He shows himself tender toward mothers. Multitudes have gathered from all over the nation. He ordains twelve apostles to do as he has done.

See how all these themes will now converge upon him. He comes down to a house, a multitude presses in upon him, but this time it is infested with a poisonous element, the *scribes,* who seek to malign and destroy him. All is building in pitch, all these various elements form the foundation to the next episode in chapter three, where all comes to a climax.

The twelve, having been called on the mount, now go down to a house for a meal and a rest with Jesus, where a new challenge stands before them, Christ is faced by an abusive mob formed by the scribes. Here is the poisonous result of the Pharisees and Herodians' counsel against him earlier, when they took offence at his healing on the sabbath, which now manifests itself.

THERE CAME ONE RUNNING

Here the pharisees use the scribes to do their dirty work. Matthew shows us the prime troublemakers were the Pharisees.

Now as we have established, his mother and his brothers are with him, as they had been with him on the mountain, where a number of his cousins or brothers had been appointed among the number of the other apostles—James the less, and Jude, Matthew and as we have proposed, Simon Zelotes. This is important to our understanding this passage, as we must observe the critical fact that his brothers are with him as part of the apostles' band. *They do not come from somewhere else.* As his brothers are with him so is his mother, and one might assume his sister Salome, accompanying her sons, of whom she has great ambitions.

Immediately following the appointment of his apostles Mark writes,

And they went into an house.

They have come down from the mountain to a settled area, where people live. But as sometimes happens when Christ has been up a mountain, a needy crowd forms down below, seeking some favours, or an argument, so that they cannot eat bread, take shelter and relax, as had been intended. They see him arrive with his followers, and gather quickly about him. Here the more so as there is this hostile element.

And the multitude comes together again, so that they could not so much as eat bread.

As we saw, there is this growing threat hidden in a crowd that the disciples would have come to fear and be wary, the crowds pressing upon them so they could not go freely or rest, or that they could be separated from one another, or that could prove a danger, insomuch that even a boat was prepared in case of such an eventuality. But now the crowd is pressing in, but with a new factor, it now has an element of aggression buried within it in the calumny of the scribes. Luke 11:29, describes the crowds as "thickly gathered together," and in 12:1, "an innumerable multitude of people had gathered together so that they *trampled* one another." Now here we come to that point where Jesus is now separated in this crowd from his friends and family. What they had feared was coming to pass.

And when his friends heard of it, they went out to lay hold on him: for they said, "He is beside himself!"

His friends are in the house, and they *heard* of it, that is they heard the tumult outside the house, they realize Jesus is not with them but out there in the midst of an angry mob, as the following verses show there is a hostile crowd driven by the scribes and pharisees. Now the word for "beside himself" is *existemi*, meaning he is *displaced*, *thrown out of position*. It can also mean *insane*. Our Bibles translate it, "he is beside himself." Typically it is read here as if he is crazy, or out of his mind, but the context shows we must take it as a *physical displacement*, we know Jesus was not insane or lacking in self-control, although it is granted that going into a hostile crowd could be considered as crazy. But he is no ordinary person. Here however he is separated from his own by a crowd, he is physically *displaced*. His friends, and his mother, who are now in the house realize he is separated in a hostile crowd, and go out to help him. As we have seen they have been beset by great multitudes, into houses where no one can enter in because of the press, where desperate people even rip roofing off houses to get to Christ. They are separated from the presence of Christ, and they feel nervous. They want to lay hold of him and rescue him away from the crowd. They are fearful of the crowd, because the scribes are stirring up opposition to him, saying evil things. Now at this point one might suppose Jesus could be rescued from the crowd by his friends and family, but this is not the case, for as we shall see Jesus will actually rescue the crowd.

And the scribes which came down from Jerusalem said, "He has Beelzebub, and by the prince of the devils casts he out devils."

Jesus is not phased by this devilish hostility and calumny, as is his disciples, although he takes it with deadly seriousness. He calls them unto him, and speaks to the crowd in parables. In Mark 1:22 they were astonished at his doctrine: for he had taught them as one that had authority, and *not as the scribes*, this is to be displayed here again.

And he called them unto him, and said unto them in parables, "How can Satan cast out Satan? And if a kingdom be divided against itself, that kingdom cannot stand. And if a house be divided against itself, that house cannot stand. And if Satan rise up against himself, and be divided, he cannot stand, but has an end. No man can enter into a strong man's house, and spoil his goods, except he will first bind the strong man; and then he will spoil his house. Verily I say unto you, All sins shall be forgiven unto the sons of men, and blasphemies

JESUS MASTERS THE MULTITUDE

wherewith soever they shall blaspheme: But he that shall blaspheme against the Holy Ghost has never forgiveness, but is in danger of eternal damnation:" Because they said, He has an unclean spirit.

Here, where the scribes are seeking to divide Christ from his people, Jesus points out that a house divided cannot stand. He speaks strong fearsome words to the opposers, and those who may be swayed by them, threatening eternal damnation. Observe this happens here where Jesus is separated from his family in the midst of this hostile crowd. He is being accused by this mob of witchcraft or wizardry. Moses said, in Leviticus 19:31, "Regard not them that have familiar spirits, neither seek after wizards, to be defiled by them." and in Exodus 22:18, "You shall not suffer a witch to live." Naturally his mother and brothers are afraid for him and themselves.

Matthew, in chapter 12, adds other points to this episode. Jesus discourses to this crowd on making the tree good, for a tree is known by its fruit, that a good man out of his heart brings forth good things, yet the pharisees are a brood of vipers, bringing forth evil things out of their hearts, who demand a sign, but Jesus says the only sign given will be that of Jonah, and he adds the men of Nineveh will rise up in judgment with this generation, as also will the queen of the south as a greater than Jonah and Solomon was here. He teaches on the infestation of seven other wicked spirits coming back to their house, as being the state of that generation. Here he is being sharp with them. Luke also adds, in this same context, the phrase, Luke 11:23, "He that is

THERE CAME ONE RUNNING

not with me is against me: and he that gathers not with me scatters."

There came then his brothers and his mother, and, standing without, sent unto him, calling him.

His brothers and mother are *standing without the crowd or the house*. His mother and brothers, that is, his disciples, venture out to the crowd to Jesus, calling to him and sending to him. They are seeking for him because he has been separated from him.

And the multitude sat about him, and they said unto him, "Behold, your mother and your brothers without seek for you."

The devilish attack has been overcome. The crowd severely and suitably chastised, are now tender toward his mother and brothers. The scribes have melted away. The crowd are said to have "sat down about him," they are changed from an active standing hostility to a resting, attentive docility. Now Jesus affirms the crowd. He has laid down the law, now he brings the gospel.

And he answered them, saying, "Who is my mother, or my brothers?" And he looked round about on them which sat about him, and said, "Behold my mother and my brothers! For whosoever shall do the will of God, the same is my brother, and my sister, and mother."

The crowd have seen his mother and his brothers, his family, he now includes the crowd in his family. In all this he displays absolute mastery and love. He leads the crowd like a bull on a leash. In asking "Who is my mother and my brothers?" he is addressing his family as well as the crowd. As if to say, "See there is my

JESUS MASTERS THE MULTITUDE

mother and brothers, you too can be! By doing the will of God you are also my brother, my sister, my mother."

Again Luke, in 11:27-28, supplies further details of a woman, who, in an obvious response to Jesus' focus on his mother and brothers cries, "And it came to pass, as he spake these things, a certain woman of the company (the common people) lifted up her voice, and said unto him, 'Blessed is the womb that bare you, and the paps which you have sucked!' " To which he makes his response, "But he said, 'Yea rather, (yea doubtless or nay surely) blessed are they that hear the word of God, and keep it.' " This is in accordance to what Luke recorded earlier, of which his mother would have heartily agreed, when Mary heard the angel Gabriel, and replied, in 1:38, "And Mary said, Behold the handmaid of the Lord; be it unto me according to your word."

Clearly his family have not made a sudden appearance to correct Jesus, as if they were worried about his mental health, they have not arrived coincidentally at the same time as the scribes. He is not rejecting his mother and brothers for the crowd. Here we are not seeing a separation from his family or a concerned objection to him by them, as many think, and he is not judging them at all. They are with him as part of the apostolic group, and they are afraid for him because of the multitude, which had become an angry mob.

His mother and brothers are actually doing the will of God, they are and have been following the Messiah. The brothers have just been appointed apostles with the others. The Virgin Mary was a faithful godly woman, she had heard the angel Gabriel, "He shall be great, and shall be called the Son of the Highest: and the Lord God shall give unto him the throne of his father David: And he shall reign over the house of Jacob for ever; and of his kingdom there shall be no end." She had pondered and kept these divine words in her heart. She would have discussed this with her family. She had found Jesus in the temple discussing with the elders. She had said to the servants at Cana, "Whatsoever he says to you, do it!" They had witnessed great miracles and the casting out of devils. They were on his side, they were accompanying him. After the marriage at Cana he went down to Capernaum, he, *and his mother,* and his brothers, and his disciples: and they continued there not many days—here we see his mother accompanied him on his travels. Luke 23:49 shows all the women that followed him followed him from the beginning, *from* Galilee, to the end, at the cross, standing afar off, beholding the crucifixion, among whom was the Virgin, and his sister Salome. He had rung in an errant brother in Matthew, the son of Alphaeus. He was restored to his brothers and mother and father. We have seen that a number of Jesus' apostles are members of his family, his brothers or cousins, James the less, Jude, Matthew, perhaps even Simon the Zealot. If he had healed Simon's wife's mother, his own mother would naturally be with him and supportive of him. His mother would have followed him with that inner group. So his family are with him among the apostles, and support him.

So here outside of the house, Jesus appears to be

JESUS MASTERS THE MULTITUDE

thrown out of position, away from his family and friends, his family are concerned for him, but being displaced in the hostile crowd, he turns the tide in the crowd and tames the errant multitude, and in doing so brings others *into* his family. Jesus appears to need rescuing, for they said, "he is beside himself, he is *displaced*." The crowd itself, which for two chapters has followed him with great expectation, growing in size and coming from everywhere, is also in danger of being displaced *from* Christ by the malice of the scribes, but he turns the balance and rescues it.

It is a wondrous masterful thing how Jesus treats this multitude. He turns them from a vicious group by the means of this sudden and tender appearance of his mother and brothers seeking for him at the edge of the crowd, where he places the attention upon them, together with his words, "Who is my mother, or my brothers?" His precious family form a kind of parable or sermon to the crowd, whom he presents to them as a kind of object lesson. Here he shows himself as the Lord.

Then it says, "And he looked round about on them which sat about him," The whole crowd are sitting, gathered in with his gaze, as he waits for them to hear, and then he says, "Behold my mother and my brothers! For whosoever shall do the will of God, the same is my brother, and my sister, and mother." Here is not a denial of his family, but an affirmation, a tender recognition of them as those who do the will of God, "Whatever he says to you do it," Mary had said, but it was also a recognition of the multitude, with a gathering *into* his family, a *welcoming* into a family. As he had come to restore Matthew to his family he now brings in the multitude. It is a conversion of a crowd. It is like what Paul called the "grafting into the olive tree," here not into the tribes of Israel but into the very family of Christ himself. In doing this he completely disarms his opponents. Jesus is the Israel of God.

When Paul tells us to "stand fast" in his epistles, he uses the word *stayko*. This word is derived from the word *histemi*, which according to *Thayer's Lexicon* means to stand in the presence of others, in the midst, before judges, before members of the Sanhedrin, to be kept intact (of family, a kingdom,) to escape in safety, to uphold or sustain the authority or force of anything, to set or place in a balance. Now this same word forms the basis for the word used by his brothers, but in its opposing sense, it is *ex-istemi*, the *ex* turns it into the opposite of *histemi*, in that they said "he is thrown out of position, he is displaced." But here we see that Jesus is not displaced at all, he stands before his judges, he keeps his family intact, his kingdom intact, he sustains his authority, he changes the balance of opposing forces, and judges his enemies. His brothers think he is thrown to the lions, but Jesus turns the crowd into a purring house cat. Jesus shows us what it means to stand fast. Here are not awkward disparate elements but a concise and cohesive flow of events. In this way we can understand this episode, and appreciate the words in John 7:45-46, "Then came the officers to the chief priests and Pharisees; and they said unto them, Why have ye not brought him? The officers answered,

JESUS MASTERS THE MULTITUDE

Never man spake like this man!"

Luke recounts the same events as Mark, that had occurred after the calling of his apostles in an extraordinary scene in chapter 6. He describes how Christ had been out on a mountain to pray all night, and when it was day he called his disciples, and of them he chose twelve, whom he named apostles. Then it was said he came down with them and stood in the plain, and the company of his disciples, and a great multitude of people out of all Judea and Jerusalem, and from the sea coast of Tyre and Sidon, which came to hear him and to be healed of their diseases, and they that were vexed with unclean spirits, and they were healed. So we have this extraordinary tableau, or panorama picture of Christ, a great gathering of his apostles and the multitude, that is reminiscent of John's vision in the Revelation 11:4:

> And I heard the number of them which were sealed: and there were sealed an hundred and forty and four thousand of all the tribes of the children of Israel. Of the tribe of Juda were sealed twelve thousand, etc. After this I beheld, and, lo, a great multitude, which no man could number, of all nations, and kindreds, and people, and tongues, stood before the throne, and before the Lamb, clothed with white robes, and palms in their hands.

Jesus had told his apostles, "Ye are they which have continued with me in my temptations. And I appoint unto you a kingdom, as my Father has appointed unto me; that you may eat and drink at my table in my kingdom, and sit on thrones judging the twelve tribes of Israel."

After this Luke writes that Christ then lifted up his

THERE CAME ONE RUNNING

eyes on his disciples and beginning with, "Blessed be you poor, for yours is the kingdom of God," he discourses on the path of love from a pure heart. Finally he likens, in verses 47-49 those who comes to him, and hear his sayings, and does them, as like a man which built an house, dug deep, and laid the foundation on a rock, so that when the flood arose, the stream beating upon that house, could not shake it, whereas those who did not, who built the foundation upon the earth, fell into a great ruin.

It is as the prophet foretold, "the people that walked in darkness have seen a great light: they that dwell in the land of the shadow of death, upon them has the light shined."

20. One Come Late

> How shall we escape, if we neglect so great salvation; which at the first began to be spoken by the Lord, and was confirmed unto us by them that heard him; God also bearing them witness, both with signs and wonders, and with diverse miracles, and gifts of the Holy Ghost, according to his own will?
> —*Hebrews 2:3-4*

WE HAVE SEEN how John has confirmed the gospel of Mark. Now we will see how Peter confirms the writings of Paul.

Galatians 2:7 shows us that "the gospel of the circumcision was unto Peter." Peter, writing, in the first instance to his Hebrew friends, would say in 2 Peter 3:15-16.

> And account that the longsuffering of our Lord is salvation; even as our beloved brother Paul also according to the wisdom given unto him has written unto you; As also in all his epistles, speaking in them of these things; in which are some things hard to be understood, which they that are unlearned and unstable wrest, as they do also the other scriptures, unto their own destruction.

Here Peter says that Paul, the apostle to the Gentiles, has written "unto you," that is to Peter's commission, *the circumcision*, the Hebrews. All Paul's other letters are addressed to Greek and Roman Gentiles, and what remains then is this epistle which, indeed and in extra measure, has Peter's word in describing the grand theme of this letter of Paul as, "the longsuffering of our

Lord is salvation." Christ tastes death for every man in order that we might be saved—this happens to be the overriding theme of the epistle to the Hebrews.

Paul heard the gospel after an encounter with Christ himself, Acts 9:2, 22:6.

> And as he journeyed, he came near Damascus: and suddenly there shined round about him a light from heaven: And he fell to the earth, and heard a voice saying to him, "Saul, Saul, why do you persecute me?" And he said, "Who are you, Lord?" And the Lord said, "I am Jesus whom you persecute: it is hard for you to kick against the pricks." And he trembling and astonished said, "Lord, what will you have me to do?" And the Lord said to him, "Arise, and go into the city, and it shall be told you what you must do." And the men which journeyed with him stood speechless, hearing a voice, but seeing no man. And Saul arose from the earth; and when his eyes were opened, he saw no man: but they led him by the hand, and brought him into Damascus. And he was three days without sight, and neither did eat nor drink.

In Galatians 2:2 we read of how he later went up, after some years, by revelation, to the other apostles, "privately to them which were of reputation, lest by any means I should run, or had run, in vain." Here they saw that the gospel was committed unto him also, and he was received into the fellowship of the apostles, Galatians 2:6-9:

> But of these who seemed to be somewhat . . . in conference added nothing to me: But contrariwise, when they saw that the gospel of the uncircumcision was committed unto me, as the gospel of the circumcision was unto Peter; (For he that wrought effectually in Peter to the apostleship of the circumcision, the same was mighty in me toward the Gentiles:) And when James, Cephas, and John, who seemed to be pillars,

ONE COME LATE

perceived the grace that was given to me, they gave to me and Barnabas the right hands of fellowship; that we should go to the heathen, and they to the circumcision.

Now let us sit this passage alongside our rather complicated text, Hebrews 2:3-4:

> How shall we escape, if we neglect so great salvation; which at the first began to be spoken by the Lord, and was confirmed unto us by them that heard him; God also bearing them witness, both with signs and wonders, and with divers miracles, and gifts of the Holy Ghost, according to his own will?

Here it is easy to assume the writer is saying he has been converted under the ministry of the twelve apostles, but we will see this is not the case. Here the writer is saying that he was not one who heard the Lord *at the first*, in other words, from the beginning. Those who had heard from the first had heard the Lord speaking of "so great salvation." This is the twelve apostles who had been with him from the beginning, according to which credential Matthias was added to their number in Acts 1. Now the writer also says that as they had borne witness with signs and wonders and gifts of the Holy Spirit, so also had he, as evidenced by the phrase "as also." God *also* bore them witness, that is the twelve, as had been borne to the writer of the epistle.

Paul writes to the Corinthians:

> For I delivered to you first of all that which I also received, how that Christ died for our sins according to the scriptures; And that he was buried, and that he rose again the third day according to the scriptures: And that he was seen of Cephas, then of the twelve: After that, he was seen of above five

hundred brothers at once; of whom the greater part remain unto this present, but some are fallen asleep. After that, he was seen of James; then of all the apostles. And last of all he was seen of me also, as of one born out of due time. For I am the least of the apostles, that am not meet to be called an apostle, because I persecuted the church of God. But by the grace of God I am what I am: and his grace which was bestowed upon me was not in vain; but I laboured more abundantly than they all: yet not I, but the grace of God which was with me. Therefore whether it were I or they, so we preach, and so you believed.

Here Christ is seen of the twelve first, "and last of all he was seen of me, as of one born out of due time," writes Paul. He also adds God's grace was bestowed upon him, as it had been with the others, in that he laboured more abundantly, the implication being as in 2 Corinthians 12, "for in nothing am I behind the very chiefest apostles, though I be nothing. Truly the signs of an apostle were wrought among you in all patience, in signs, and wonders, and mighty deeds." It is as "God *also bearing them* witness, both with signs and wonders, and with divers miracles, and gifts of the Holy Ghost, according to his own will." Here then Paul is talking of himself, who had not seen the Lord at the beginning, but as of one come late to the vineyard, through whom God had borne witness with great power — such "signs, wonders and mighty deeds" that "God also bears witness" with the other apostles. The writer is an apostle.

In the "and was confirmed unto us by them that heard him," the word *confirmed* is *bebayo-oh*. This is *not* the word for *preached / euangelidzo*, which would be the word expected to be used, of ones who are

ONE COME LATE

converted under the ministry of the apostles, as it is in 4:6 and elsewhere, "they to whom it was first *preached* entered not in because of unbelief." However *confirm / bebayo-oh* does not mean to preach the gospel, but rather to make firm and sure, establish, confirm. The confirming in the faith *follows* the preaching of the faith, it implies the hearer's previous possession of the gospel. There are instances in the epistles where we find this confirming of the believers. So here is not regarding those who have just newly heard the good news, but those who possess it already. Here we can suppose Paul, using the royal "us," as the one who is saying how he as having already possessed the gospel, as it had first come to him through Christ himself, that it was later *confirmed* unto him by "them that heard him," that is by the first apostles, those who at the first heard so great salvation—it was made firm, confirmed as the genuine article, among the apostolic circle, as indeed it was in the account we referenced in Galatians 2:6-9, where James, Peter and John perceived the grace given to him, that is, Paul. In Romans 15:8 the same word, *bebayo-oh* is used, to establish the promises, that the Gentiles might glorify God:

> Wherefore receive you one another, as Christ also received us to the glory of God. Now I say that Jesus Christ was a minister of the circumcision for the truth of God, to *confirm* the promises made unto the fathers. And that the Gentiles might glorify God for his mercy; as it is written, For this cause I will confess to you among the Gentiles, and sing unto your name.

Paul was the apostle to the Gentiles, bearing the promises of Jesus to them. The *fathers* are Abraham,

Isaac, and Jacob, the *faithful* are both believing Jew and Gentile: Acts 3:13: "The God of Abraham, and of Isaac, and of Jacob, the God of our fathers," Ezekiel 47:22-23 gives us an insight regarding the induction of strangers / gentiles into the commonwealth of Israel:

> And it shall come to pass, that you shall divide it by lot for an inheritance to you, and to the strangers that sojourn among you, which shall beget children among you: and they shall be unto you as born in the country among the children of Israel; they shall have inheritance with you among the tribes of Israel. And it shall come to pass, that in what tribe the stranger sojourns, there shall you give him his inheritance, says the Lord GOD.

As Paul's calling was to the Gentiles, the heathen, similarly the Romans were recipients of the promise given to the Fathers, which were *confirmed* to them. This *establishing* or *"confirming unto us,"* in Hebrews 2:3, that is, to Paul, then, was a recognizing of the genuineness of the word given to Paul and his calling as an apostle.

Given that Peter was the apostle to the circumcision, it was appropriate that it should be he to *precis* or confirm in his communications with the Hebrews any letter to the Hebrews from the apostle to the Gentiles, as we see in 2 Peter 3:15-16.

> As also in all his epistles, speaking in them of these things; in which are some things hard to be understood, which they that are unlearned and unstable wrest, as they do also the other scriptures, unto their own destruction.

Paul always took the gospel to the world with the view of first the Jew then the Gentile, and conversely, according to the Corinthians, Peter also held a place as

ONE COME LATE

teacher with the Greeks. "I am of Peter, I am of Paul." Paul writes in Galatians 2:7-9:

> But contrariwise, when they saw that the gospel of the uncircumcision was committed unto me, as the gospel of the circumcision was unto Peter; (For he that wrought effectually in Peter to the apostleship of the circumcision, the same was mighty in me toward the Gentiles:) And when James, Cephas, and John, who seemed to be pillars, perceived the grace that was given to me, they gave to me and Barnabas the right hands of fellowship; that we should go to the heathen, and they to the circumcision.

There is a true sense of yokefellows among the apostles in their evangelizing the world, and by the time of the final reckoning among the apostate Jews, when the division of allegiance to Christ had finally been set in upturned stone with the fall of Jerusalem, all divisions of ethnicity have become redundant, and St John, fleeing Palestine, would take over the oversight of Paul's Ephesian churches. The casual reader of this epistle would agree with that statement of Peter speaking of Paul's letter, "in which are some things hard to be understood."

We have the reference of "our brother Timothy," a close companion of Paul, in the last chapter, verse 23:

> Know you that our brother Timothy is set at liberty; with whom, if he come shortly, I will see you. Salute all them that have the rule over you, and all the saints. They of Italy salute you.

It was a time when Timothy had been released from imprisonment, he is given his freedom, he is set at liberty. Timothy is often referred to as "my son," by Paul, like Mark was to Peter. The author is surrounded by Italians, "they of Italy salute you." Now Paul was connected with Rome as having written to them and later become a prisoner there. Or perhaps it is imprisonment in the two years he was at Caesarea before being transported to Rome, see Acts 23:33, 24:23, 27. The time in Caesarea would most certainly have been put to profitable use by Paul, separate from his Greek churches, and surrounded by Romans and Hebrews, in Palestine. His friends were allowed to minister to him and were free to come unto him. Paul's companion Luke would have been at liberty here to have composed his gospel, on intimate terms with many sources in Judea, including Paul, one who had been chief inquisitor over the early believers, taking them to prison! See Acts 9:1-2. As such a prison warden he would have questioned the Christians at length regarding the facts of their faith. He would have many contacts with the earlier Christians. In either case, whether he be in Rome or Palestine, Paul would have been surrounded by Italians. Much of Luke's gospel is non-chronological, after chapter 8, it is a mix of different events, as if a compilation of different sources.

Timothy was an intimate of Paul, perhaps a fellow prisoner with Paul, and if Timothy is released, bearing the letter to the Hebrews, from Rome or Caesarea Philippi, then "if he comes" it will be as if Paul had come and seen them, in the sense of the Greek phrase "I will see you" as being *to allow one's self to be seen.* Perhaps it is that some would visit him—"I will see you." It is as he wrote in the epistle, Hebrews 13:3,

Remember them that are in bonds, as bound with them; and

them which suffer adversity, as being yourselves also in the body.

In Philippians Paul also uses that same word *bebahyosis / confirmation*. He *confirms* that the gospel has borne fruit within them also, they also "partake of my grace." Now Peter writes this same thing, in confirming *his* hearers—in saying that "this is the true grace of God in which you stand," 1 Peter 5:12:

> By Silvanus, a faithful brother unto you, as I suppose, I have written briefly, exhorting, and testifying that this is the true grace of God wherein ye stand.

Here we have a "confirming." Furthermore this Silvanus is the brother Peter used to confirm other disciples, through a letter, affirming their acceptance by God in the gospel. Now Silvanus was a disciple, companion and preacher of Paul's band, as seen in the following passage, in 2 Corinthians, 2:16-19-23:

> And to pass by you into Macedonia, and to come again out of Macedonia unto you, and of you to be brought on my way toward Judaea. When I therefore was thus minded, did I use lightness? or the things that I purpose, do I purpose according to the flesh, that with me there should be yea yea, and nay nay? But as God is true, our word toward you was not yea and nay. For the Son of God, Jesus Christ, who was preached among you by us, even by me and Silvanus and Timotheus, was not yea and nay, but in him was yea. For all the promises of God in him are yea, and in him *Amen*, unto the glory of God by us. Now he which *stablishes* us with you in Christ, and has anointed us, is God; Who has also sealed us, and given the earnest of the Spirit in our hearts. Moreover I call God for a record upon my soul, that to spare you I came not as yet unto Corinth.

Paul here is administering in large measure the

comfort of the confirmation of the faith in which these Corinthians now stand, in that it is indeed the genuine thing. He affirms the positive nature of the promises, regarding the son of God, that they are established in Christ with one another, anointed, and sealed, and given the Spirit in their hearts, all is tremendous confirmation and comfort. The word *established* in verse 21 of this passage is again our familiar word *bebayo-oh*. The word was preached among them by Paul, Timothy *and Silvanus*. That Peter would use Silvanus, a colleague of Paul, to affirm Hebrews and Greeks, in his epistle, of the grace of God in them, echoes this former time when Paul himself received a confirmation of his faith in the eyes of the other apostles. We see this dynamic relationship among the apostles, and their believers, a brotherhood, of Macedonians and Judeans, of circumcision and uncircumcision, Christ is all and in all, where they are confirmed and established in the faith. See Colossians 3:11. In the Roman world the Mediterranean was a great highway, with which close relations and communications would be frequently maintained.

The apostle Paul has seen Christ, in Galatians 2:6 we see that he knows that God is the one who has established him in Christ:

But of these who seemed to be somewhat, (whatsoever they were, it makes no matter to me: God accepts no man's person:) for they who seemed to be somewhat in conference added nothing to me:

He respects the other apostles, but he does not allow

ONE COME LATE

any to lord it over his faith and credibility, his faith in God knows no fear of men or fawning toward personalities, he lives in an equality with other believers. Christ is Lord and no other. Faithful men do not need approval, they just need the strength of their convictions. He regards other believers in an equality as well, notice from 2 Corinthians 1:21-22, "Now he which stablishes us with you in Christ, and has anointed us, is God; Who has also sealed us, and given the earnest of the Spirit in our hearts."

We are on the same level with the apostle before Christ. Furthermore Paul goes further as we see this in his teaching to us regarding teachers in 1 Corinthians 3:21-22, "Therefore let no man glory in men. For all things are yours; Whether Paul, or Apollos, or Cephas, or the world, or life, or death, or things present, or things to come; all are yours."

He says that he, along with Peter and Apollos are *theirs*. They are servants, stewards of the gospel, in all humility and debasement, verses 8-13:

Now ye are full, now you are rich, you have reigned as kings without us: and I would to God you did reign, that we also might reign with you. For I think that God has set forth us the apostles last, as it were appointed to death: for we are made a spectacle unto the world, and to angels, and to men. We are fools for Christ's sake, but you are wise in Christ; we are weak, but you are strong; you are honourable, but we are despised. Even unto this present hour we both hunger, and thirst, and are naked, and are buffeted, and have no certain dwelling place; and labour, working with our own hands: being reviled, we bless; being persecuted, we suffer it: Being defamed, we intreat: we are made as the filth of the world, and are the offscouring of all things unto this day.

We are not to regard ourselves as the *property* of other teachers, whether they are Paul, Apollos or Cephas (Peter.) Rather the teachers are gifts to us to help us in our faith. Paul tells us that ultimately it is God who is the one who establishes us—in Christ we are bebayo-ohed / established by God, verses 21-22, "Now he which stablisheth us with you in Christ, and has anointed us, is God; Who has also sealed us, and given the earnest of the Spirit in our hearts."

We are established, confirmed, God has anointed us, sealed us, given us the gift, or the earnest of the Holy Spirit. God anointed Jesus with the Holy Spirit, and in doing so he opens the way for man to be purified and made holy in repentance and baptism. This is the connection, as with Christ so also with we. The role of a Peter, Paul or Silvanus then is to affirm that God has done that very thing. Paul did not lord it over his band either, as 1 Corinthians 16:12 shows us:

> As touching our brother Apollos, I greatly desired him to come to you with the brothers: but his will was not at all to come at this time; but he will come when he shall have convenient time.

He desired Apollos to come, but left him to the freedom of his will, he does not coerce him at all. And Apollos did not feel compelled by Paul. Ministers would do well to consider this. We read of Silvanus, or Silas as he is also known, who with Judas had delivered the corrective letter to the disciples at Antioch, who after being released from that commission, chose to stay longer anyway, Acts 15:4, "Notwithstanding it pleased Silas to abide there still."

ONE COME LATE

All is freedom and equality. The work of Silas everywhere carries this character of confirming the disciples, and verse 32, "And Judas and Silas, being prophets also themselves, exhorted the brothers with many words, and confirmed them." *Confirmed* here is another word, *episterizo*. Again Paul with Silas confirming the disciples, verse 40-41, "And Paul chose Silas, and departed, being recommended by the brothers to the grace of God. And he went through Syria and Cilicia, confirming the churches."

When Paul came to Corinth alone from Athens, in Acts 18, he was in some fear at the task the city presented to him, as verse 9 shows. He had to ascertain the right approach to this large cosmopolitan city. He made friends with some Jewish tentmakers, he "went to the synagogue, and reasoned and persuaded Jews and Greeks." *Reasoned / dialegomai* has the meaning of: to think different things with one's self, mingle thought with thought, to ponder, revolve in mind, to converse, discourse with one, argue, discuss. The word *persuaded / peitho*, has the meaning of: to make friends of, to win one's favour, gain one's good will, or to seek to win one, strive to please one. This reasoning and persuading was not the gospel message. Paul did not jump straight in with the gospel, his communication up to that point was a laying a foundation of relationship and thought, as the message of Christ crucified, a stumbling block for the Jews, and foolishness to the Greeks, had not as yet been preached. It was not until his companions, Silas and Timothy had joined him that he was, verse 5, "pressed in the spirit, and testified to the Jews that

Jesus was Christ." The hostile response to the gospel, verse 6, shows that Paul's fears were quite justified, but his time of establishing friendship opened the door to Justus and Crispus, of and near the synagogue, and the Lord spoke to him to not be afraid and speak, as he had much people in that city. Here we see the encouraging and strengthening presence of Silas / Silvanus to Paul, and the spread of the gospel. To this very city we would see the influence of Peter also. See 1 Corinthians 3:22, 9:5. All is brotherhood and collegiality.

In seeking to understand these obscure odd passages in Hebrews we have opened to us the authorship of Paul and also the practise of confirmation in the early church. It is by these means that God the Father of all mercies and the God of all comfort consolidates all believers. We can take to heart Paul's word to the Corinthians, "May the God of all comfort comfort us in all our tribulation, that we may be able to comfort them which are in any trouble, by the comfort wherewith we ourselves are comforted of God."

In establishing that Paul was the author of the letter to the Hebrews, we can read it in the knowledge of the author, and we can meet it with an array of other verses from his letters, and his thinking. Knowing the author can make a big difference to understanding his writing. We can understand that one who had sat at the feet of Gamaliel, who had been intimately connected to the religious elite of that nation is writing to his people, to those who had been confirmed in the faith of the New Testament. Paul wrote in Romans chapter 9:3-5,

For I could wish that myself were accursed from Christ for

ONE COME LATE

my brothers, my kinsmen according to the flesh: who are Israelites; to whom pertain the adoption, and the glory, and the covenants, and the giving of the law, and the service of God, and the promises; whose are the fathers, and of whom as concerning the flesh Christ came, who is over all, God blessed for ever. Amen.

We can understand his love for his kinfolk, and we can set in to the context of his day, of an apostle who would soon if not already be in Rome, awaiting the judgment of Caesar, before the judgment would fall on his land. Here is one who takes seriously that warning of Christ, that that generation would not pass away until the temple and city would be destroyed by surrounding armies, as his companion Luke had declared, and that his people would need to flee at the portents which Christ had warned them. This word to his people is what Daniel had prophesied, Daniel 9:27:

> And he shall confirm the covenant with many for one week: and in the midst of the week he shall cause the sacrifice and the oblation to cease, and for the overspreading of abominations he shall make it desolate, even until the consummation, and that determined shall be poured upon the desolate.

Paul himself had been confirmed into that faith, into the New Covenant, and he is writing to the multitude of believers in Christ from among his own people in Judea, who had also been confirmed into that Covenant, and to those who had not yet believed. The prophet also says the Messiah, the Christ, causes the Old Covenant to cease, making the old Levitical practices obsolete, even an abomination, as Christ is now our sacrifice, and that this consummation, that is, complete destruction, would be poured upon "the desolate," that is those who have not been confirmed in the New Covenant, who still trust in that earthly temple, of which Christ had declared, in Matthew 23:38, "Behold, your house is left unto you desolate." This was fulfilled under the siege of Titus in the year 70. That Christ had taken all to the heavenly sanctuary, and that they must escape from the earthly, forms the burden of the letter to the Hebrews. Peter had said of Paul, that he spoke of "some things *hard to be understood*," surely a reference to the epistle to the Hebrews, where in chapter five Christ is "called of God an high priest after the order of Melchisedec. Of whom we have many things to say, and *hard to be uttered*, seeing you are dull of hearing."

The New Testament presents to us personalities and psychological observations. Knowing who wrote this letter to the Hebrews, a particular personality, of whom we are already familiar in his other writings, gives us further insight into understanding the letter.

21. Conclusion

WE FIND THEN these hidden stories of real people, friends and relations, who lived and associated with one another in an extraordinary amity and humanity. People who knew one another wrote of one another. All these letters and gospels reflect the reality of real events and real people and real happenings. We must respect and trust the narrative of Scripture and its innate integrity, in order to understand it. The scripture is no clever fabrication but a true record of real historical reality. Peter said, "we have not followed cunningly devised fables, when we made known unto you the power and coming of our Lord Jesus Christ, but were eyewitnesses of his majesty." Fiction is neat and tidy, but real life has curious and quirky details, and seeming contradictions, and the gospel accounts are full of such little details. Here we are dealing with actual events and the relations of real historical personalities; we have a real breathing community, taken up with salutations, breathing an atmosphere of mutual love, where saints assist and succour, help, lay down their own necks, bestow labour, open their houses, share imprisonment and holy kisses, and are mothers, sisters and brothers to one another, among whom the Son of God is declared as having walked in ordinary and in extraordinary ways. In understanding these things the majesty and truthfulness of the scriptures is magnified and that eternal life, which was with the Father, is manifested unto us.

www.ingramcontent.com/pod-product-compliance
Lightning Source LLC
Chambersburg PA
CBHW011522070526
44585CB00022B/2498